The Tao of Bondage

An Erotic Binding Companion

Nell Gwyn

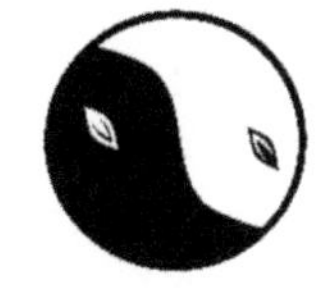

Drrty Grrl Productions

The Tao of Bondage
An Erotic Binding Companion

Drrty Grrl Productions

ISBN: 9781946732620

The Tao of Naughty series is presented by:

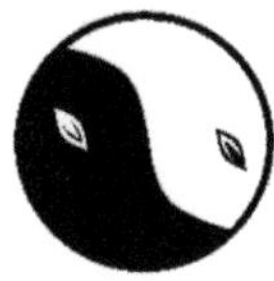

DRRTY GRRL PRODUCTIONS

Erotic Exploration & Empowerment

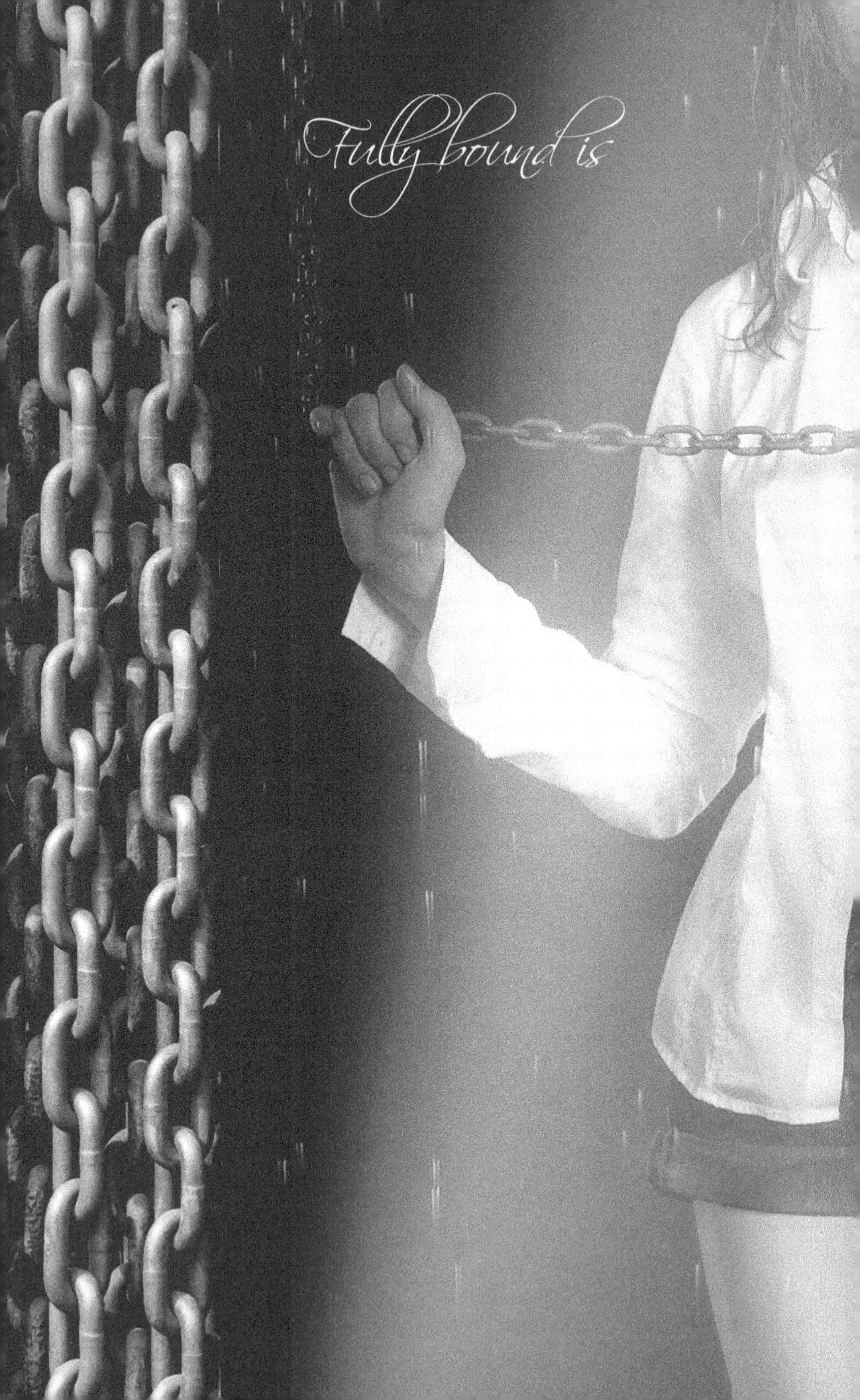
Fully bound is

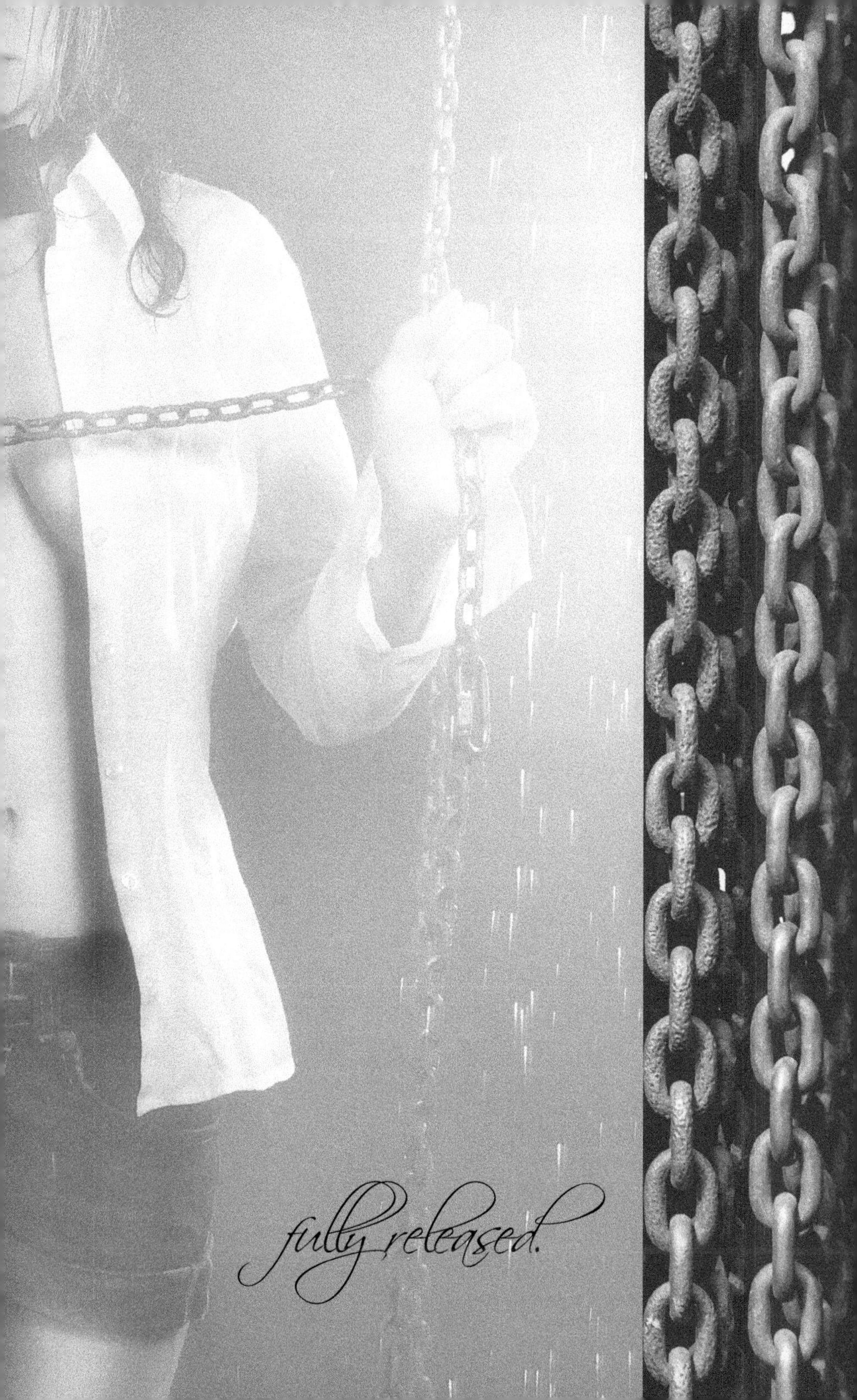
fully released.

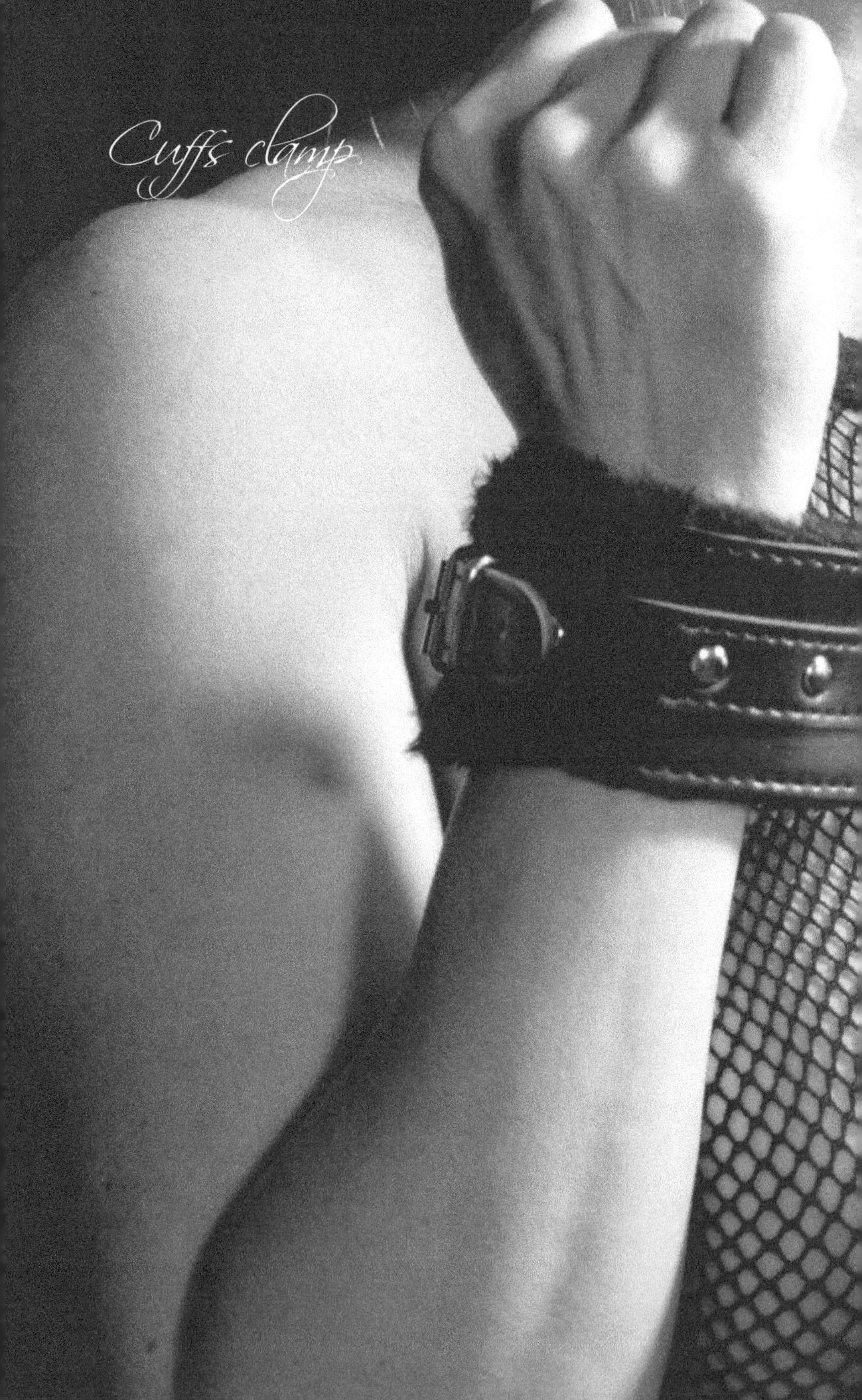
Cuffs clamp

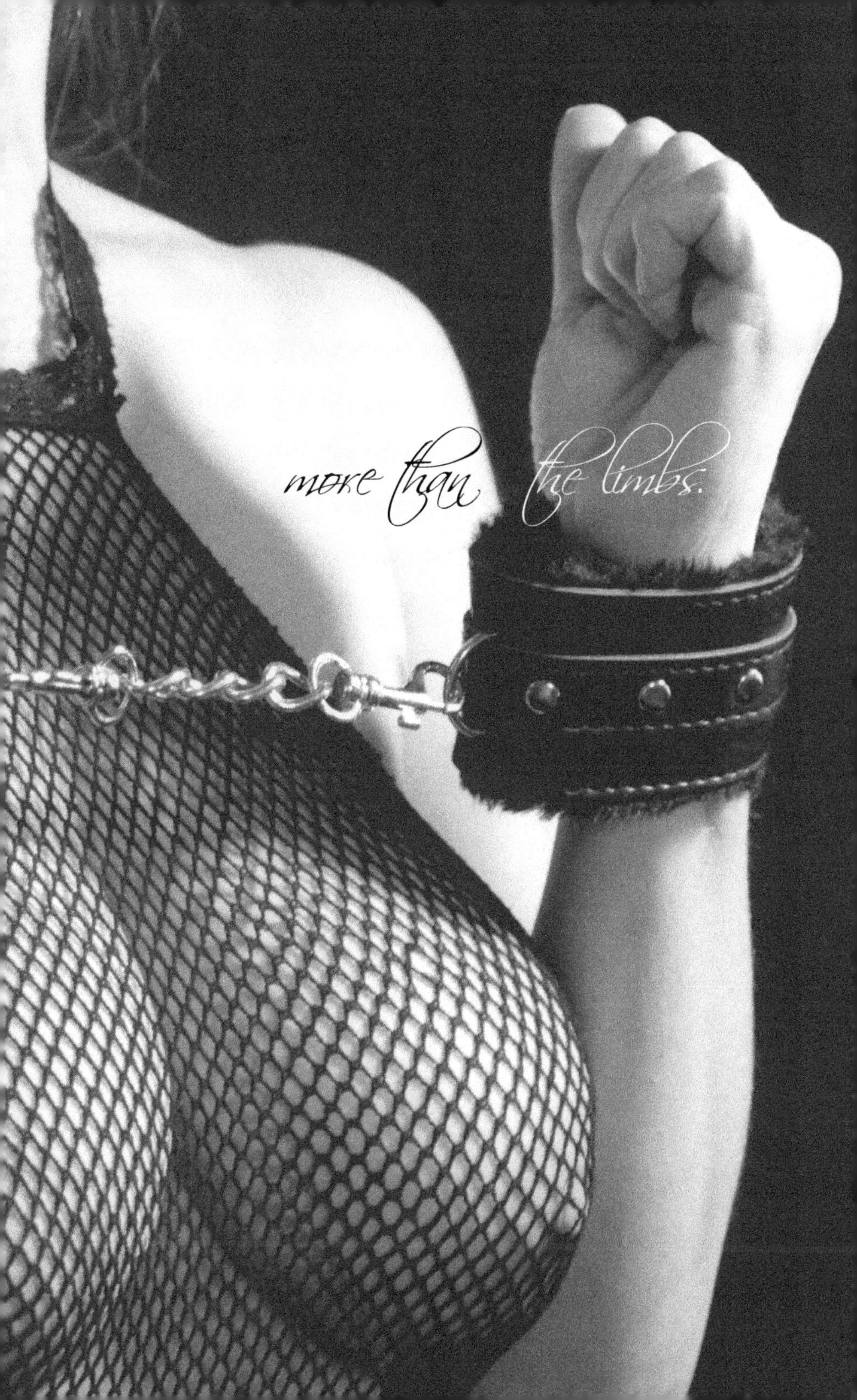

more than the limbs.

Rope is both

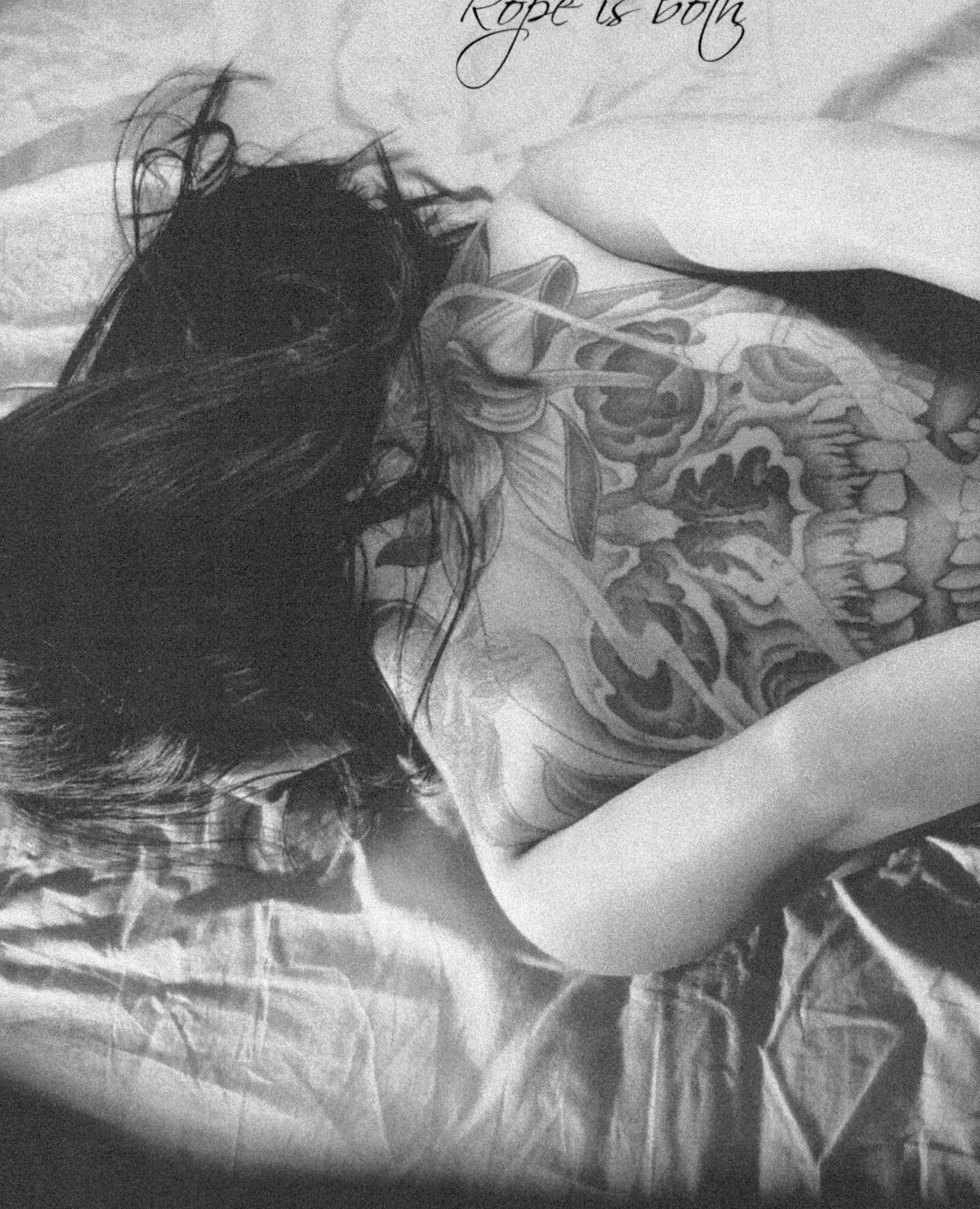

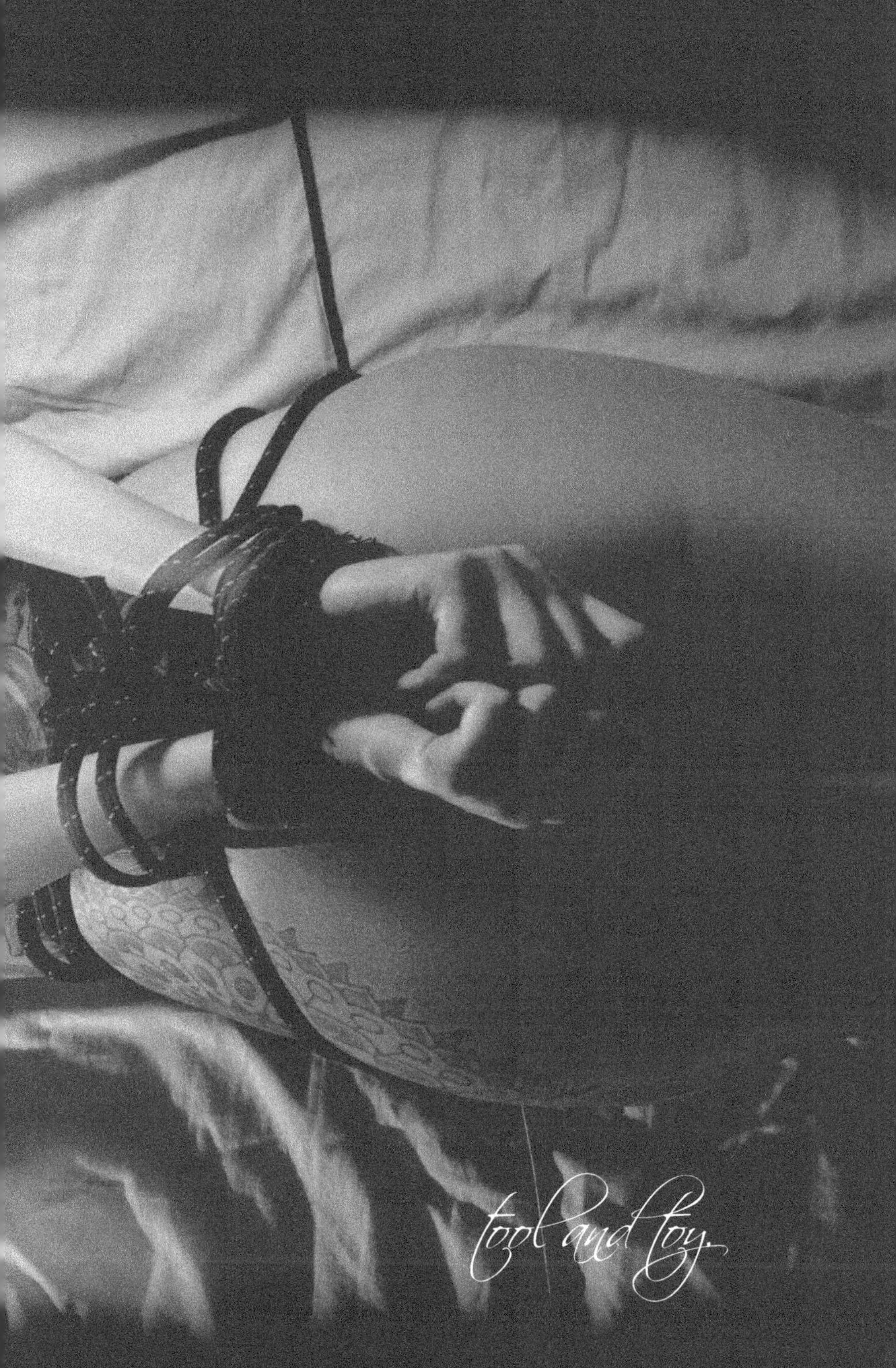
tool and toy.

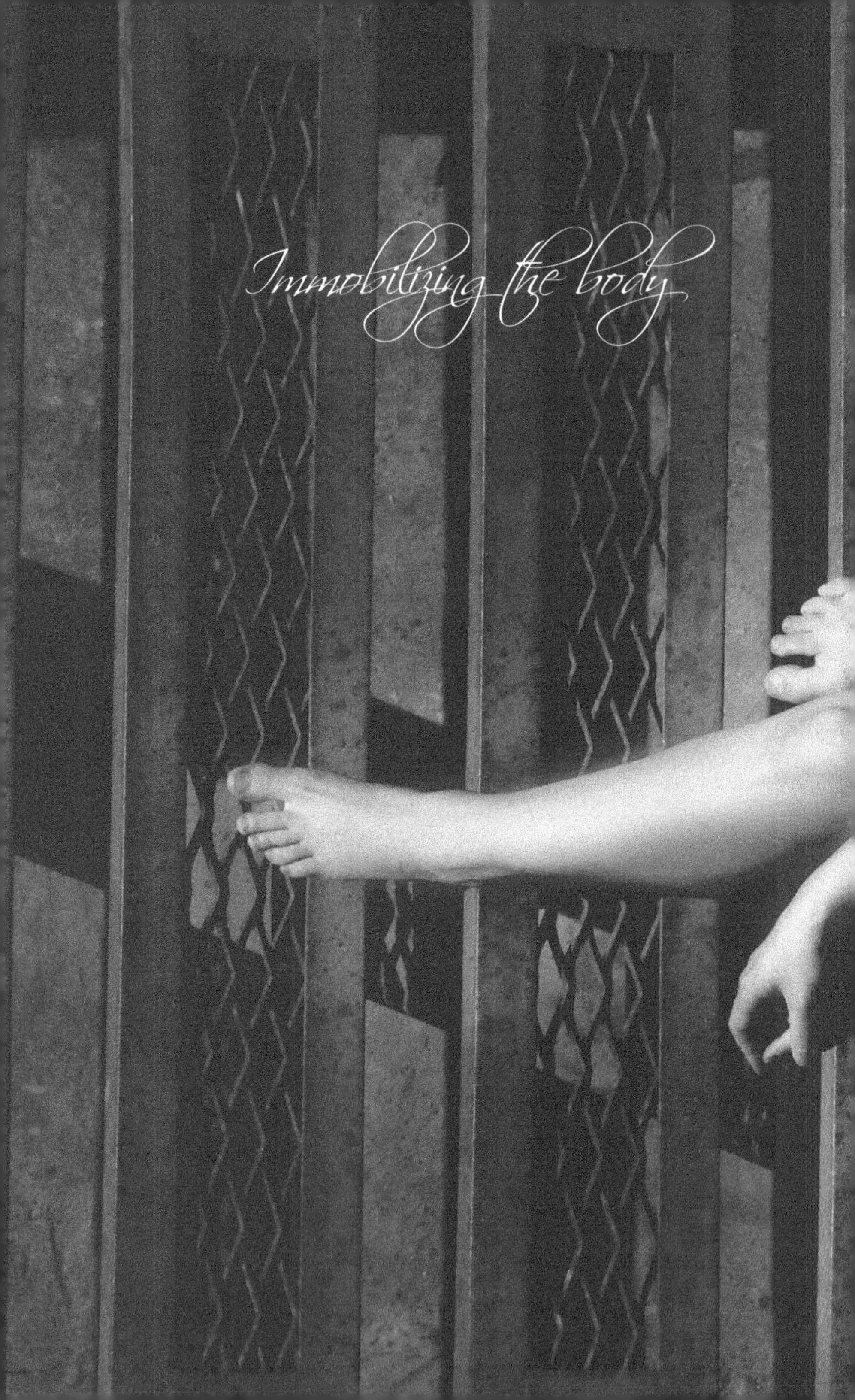

Immobilizing the body

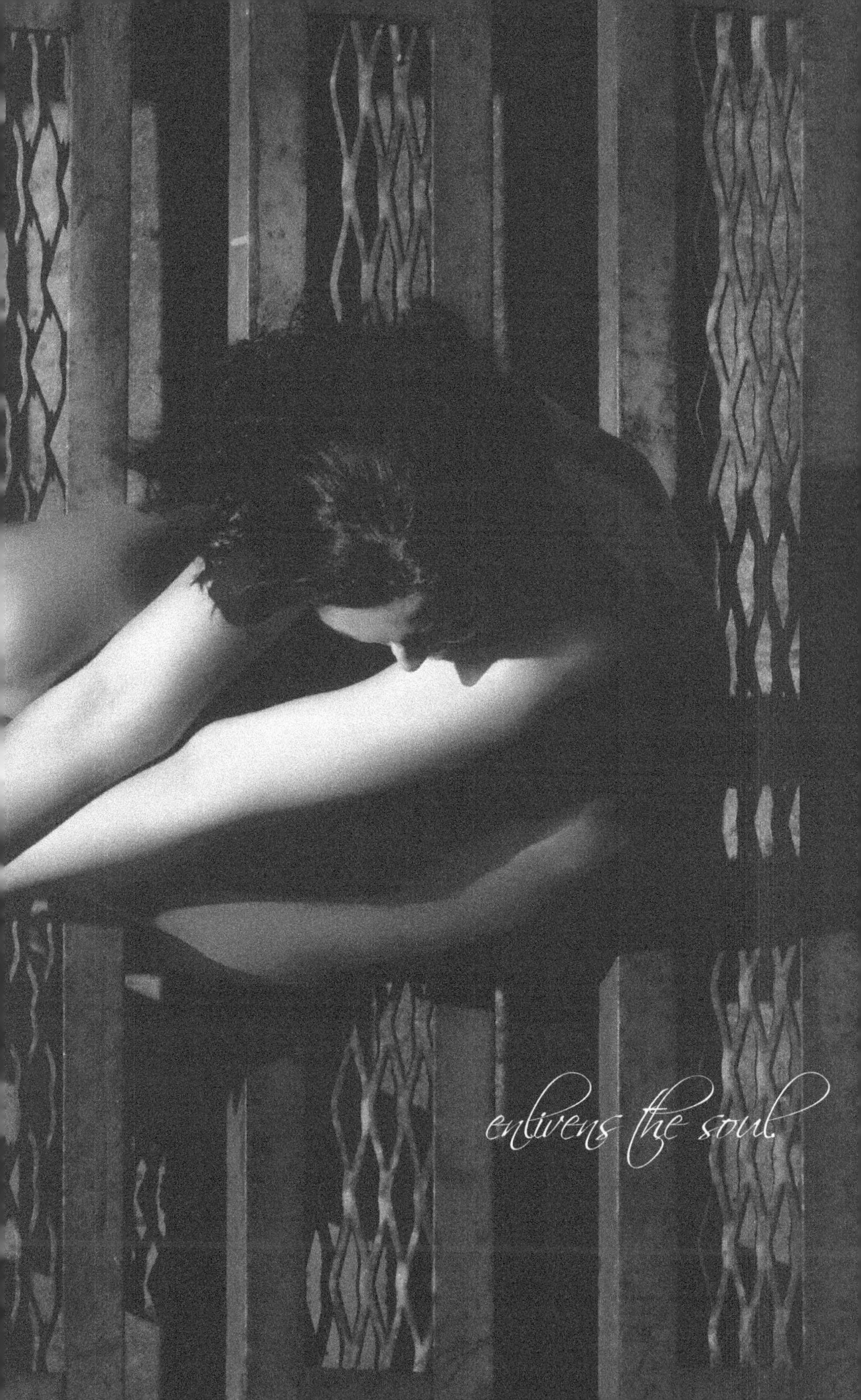
enlivens the soul.

Gags subdue

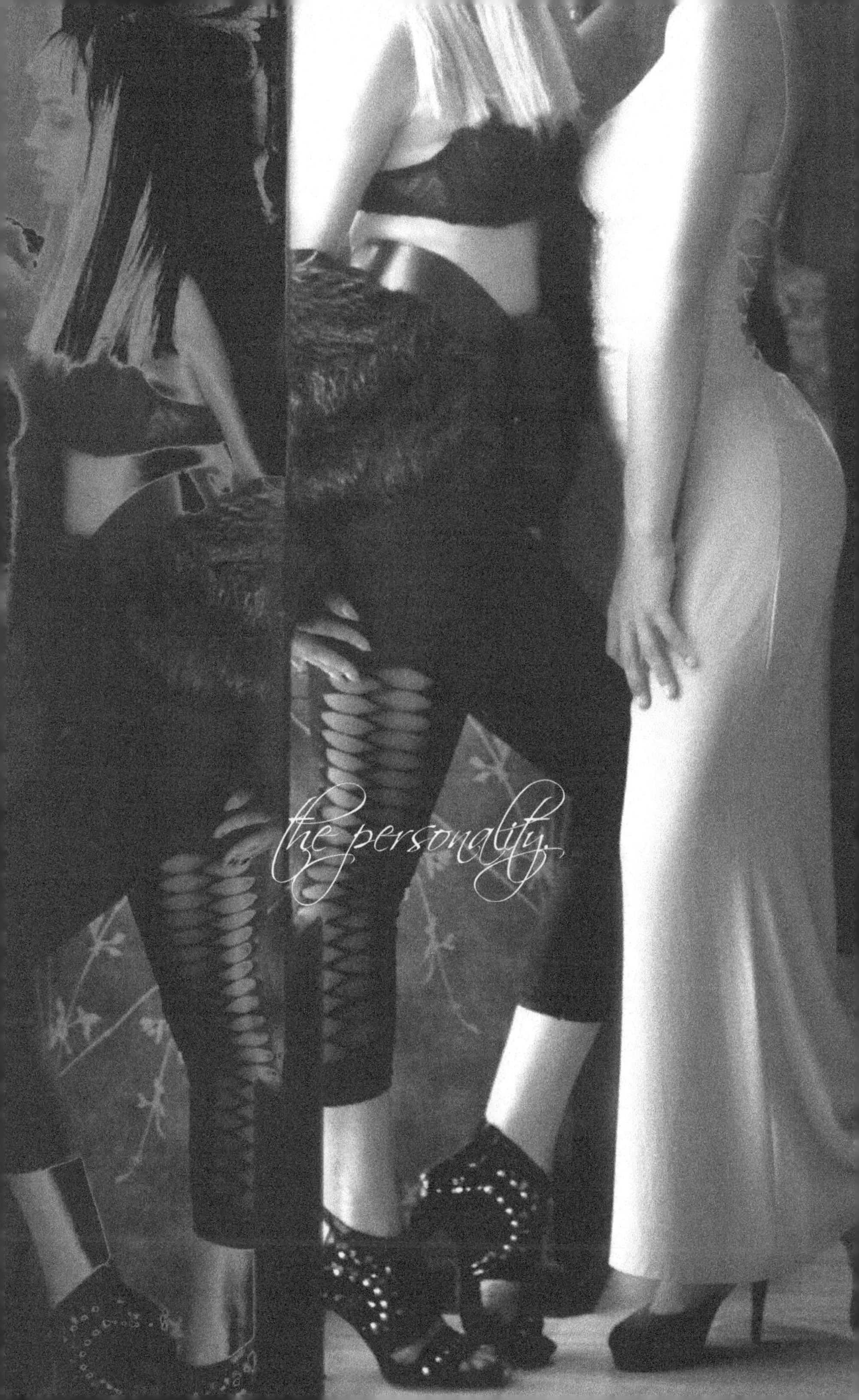
the personality.

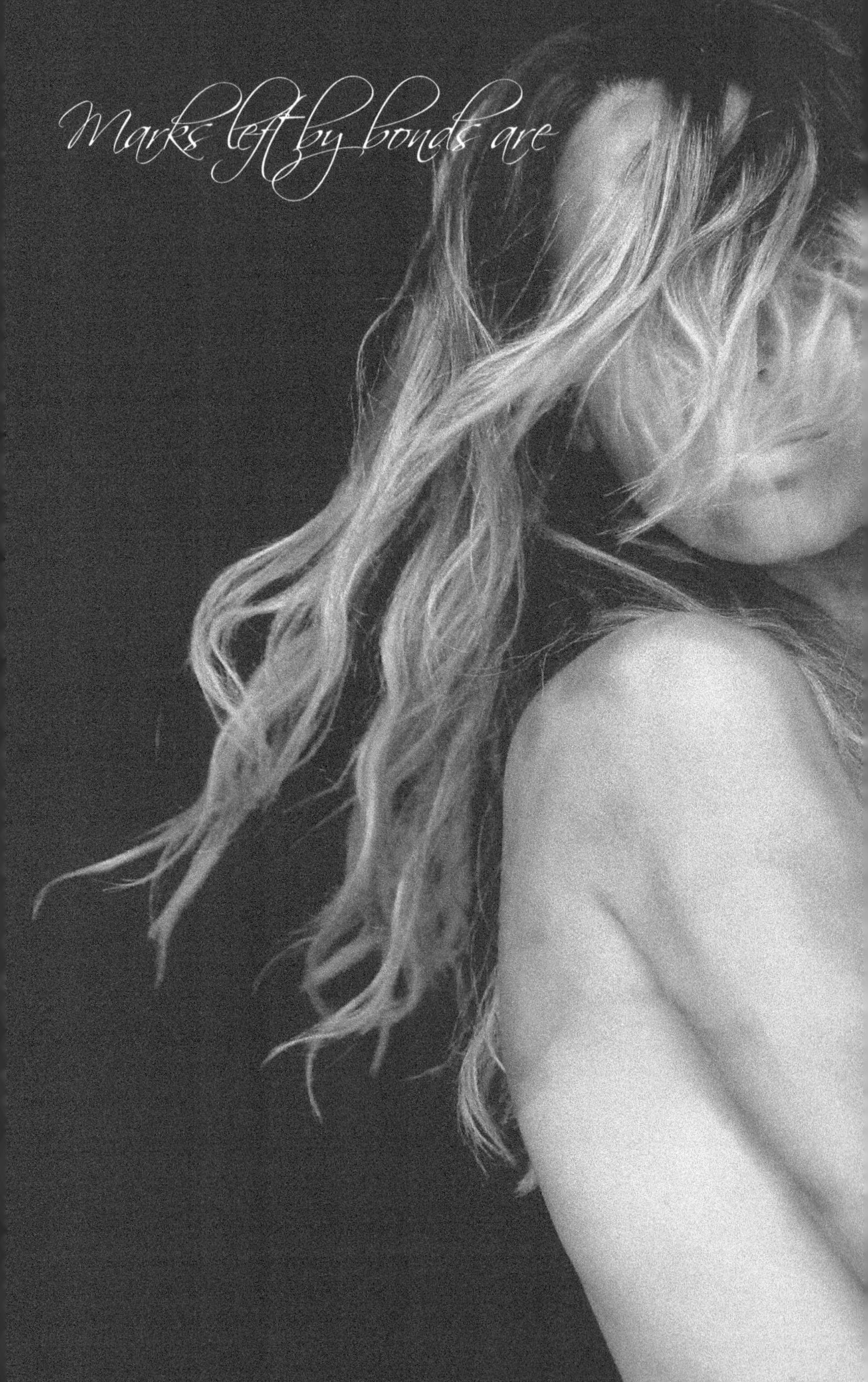
Marks left by bonds are

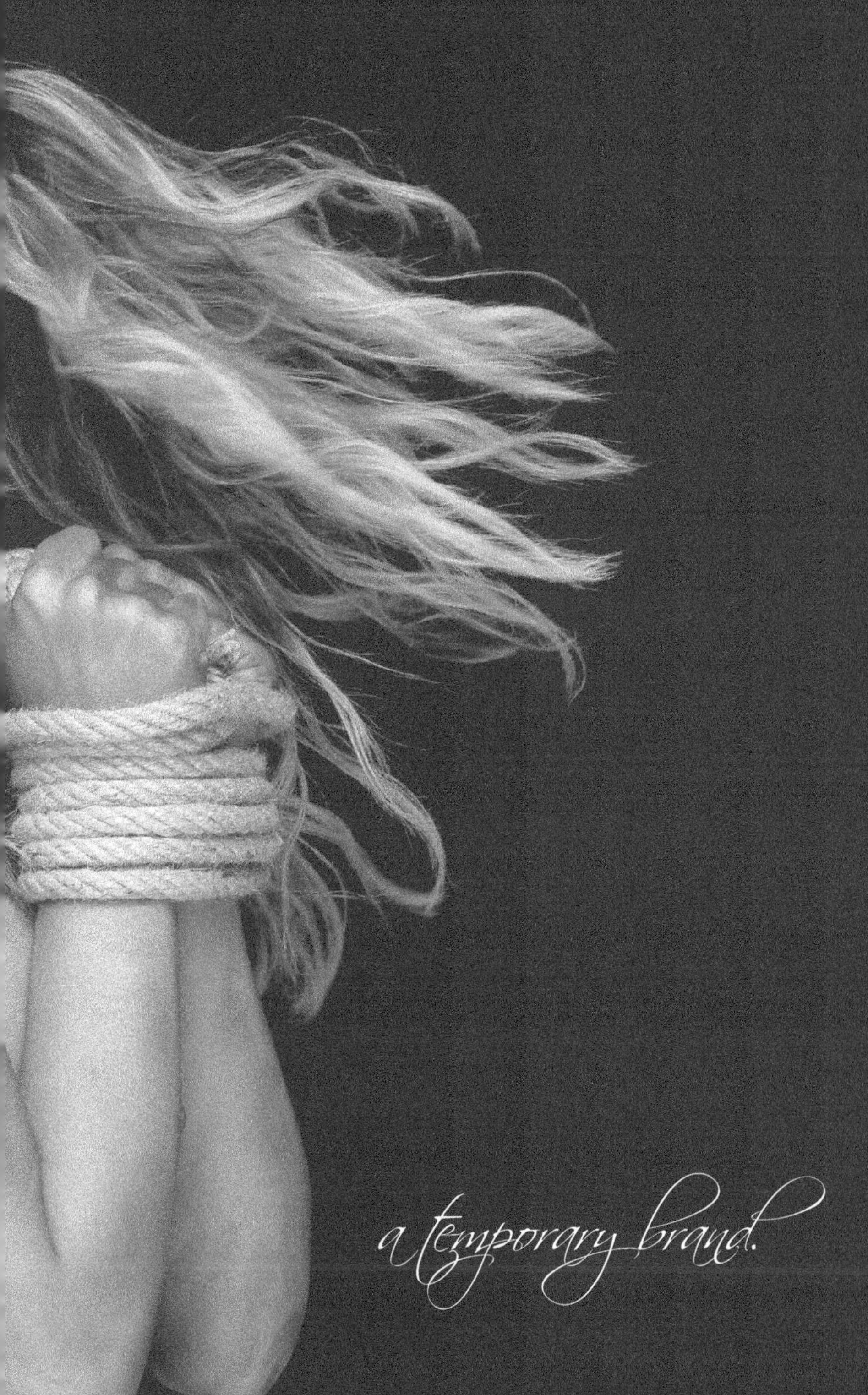
a temporary brand.

Flexibility enhances

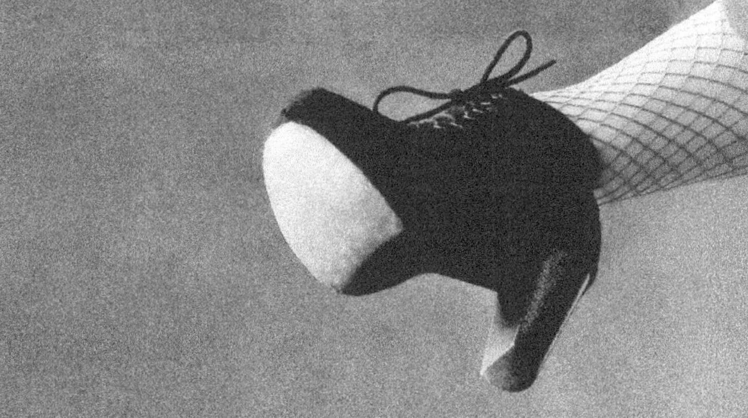

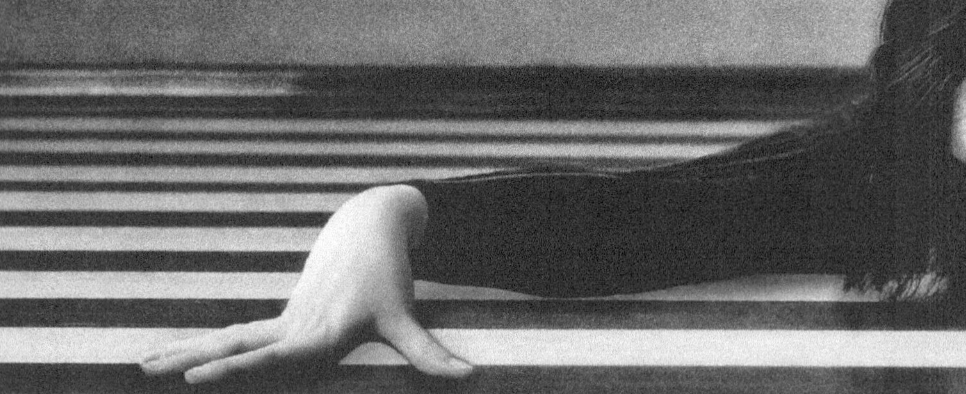

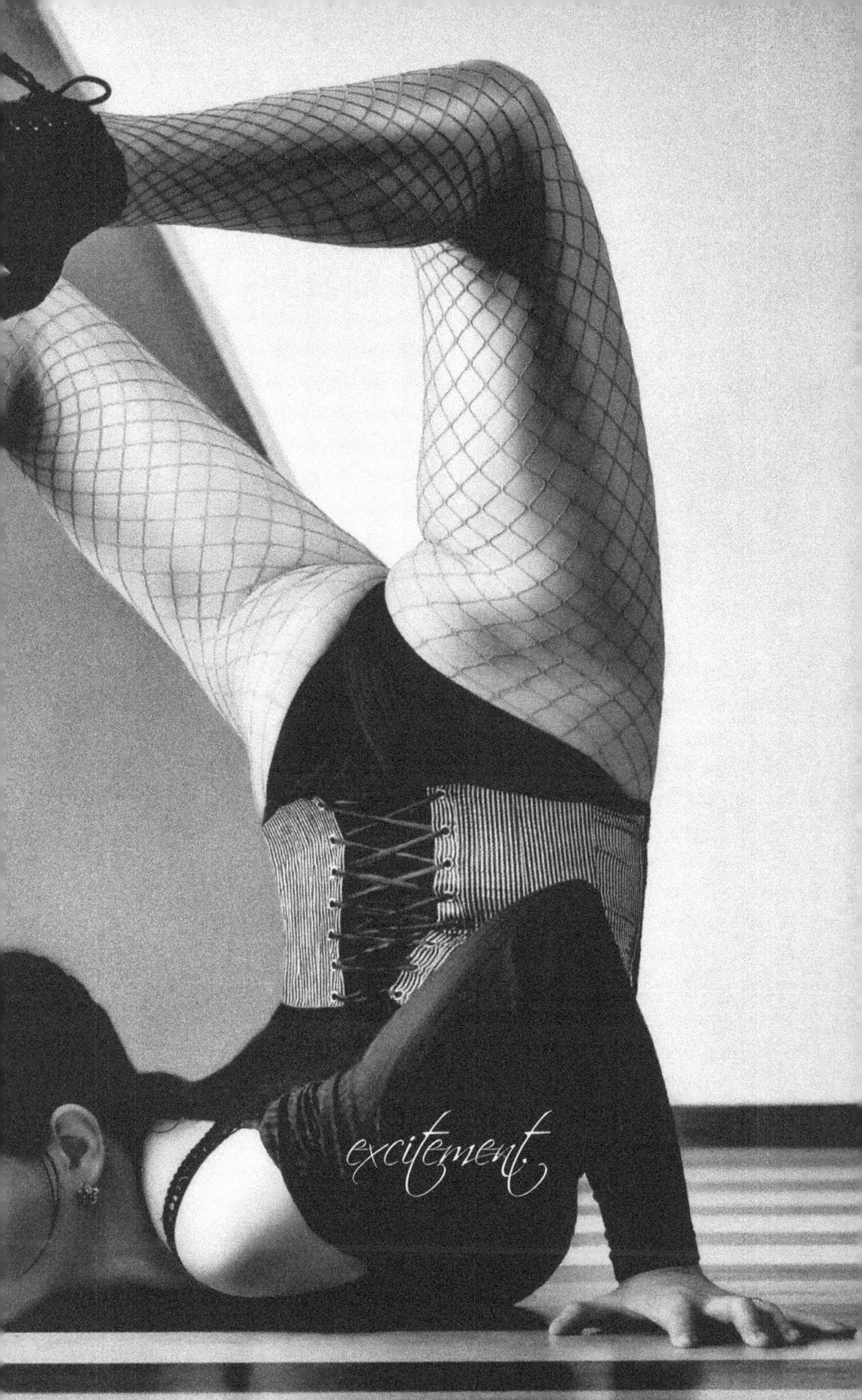
excitement.

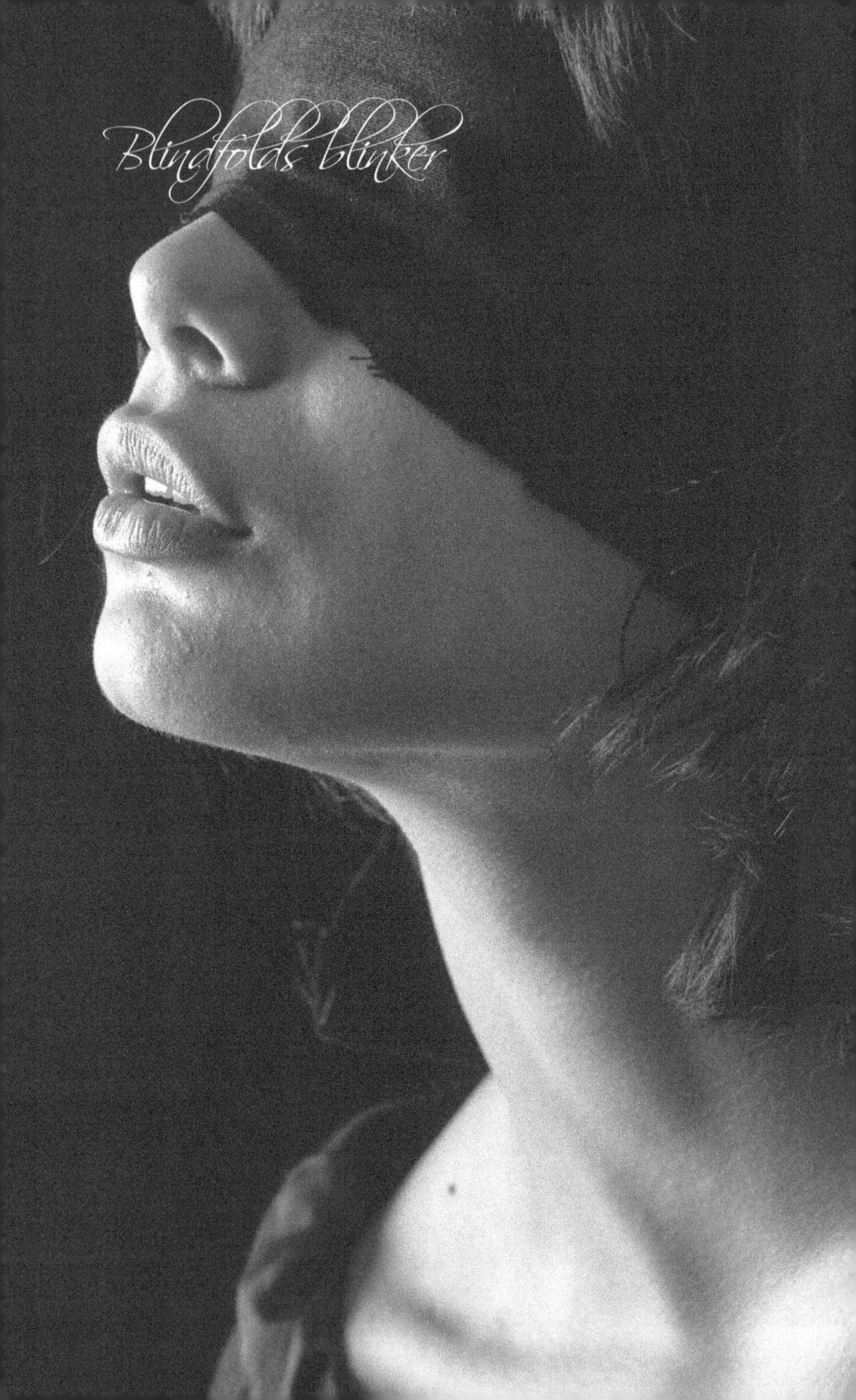

Blindfolds blinker

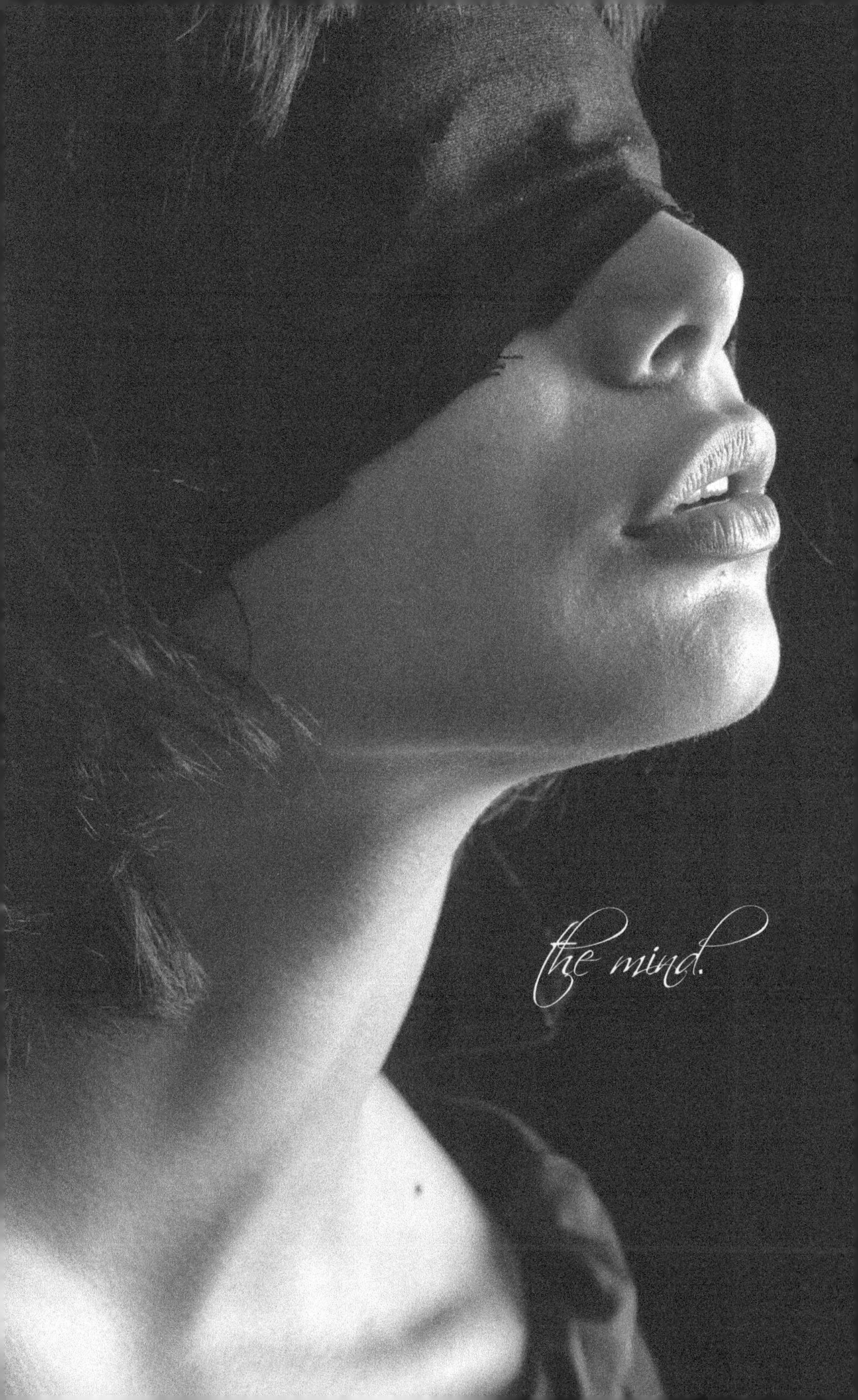

the mind.

The act of binding is

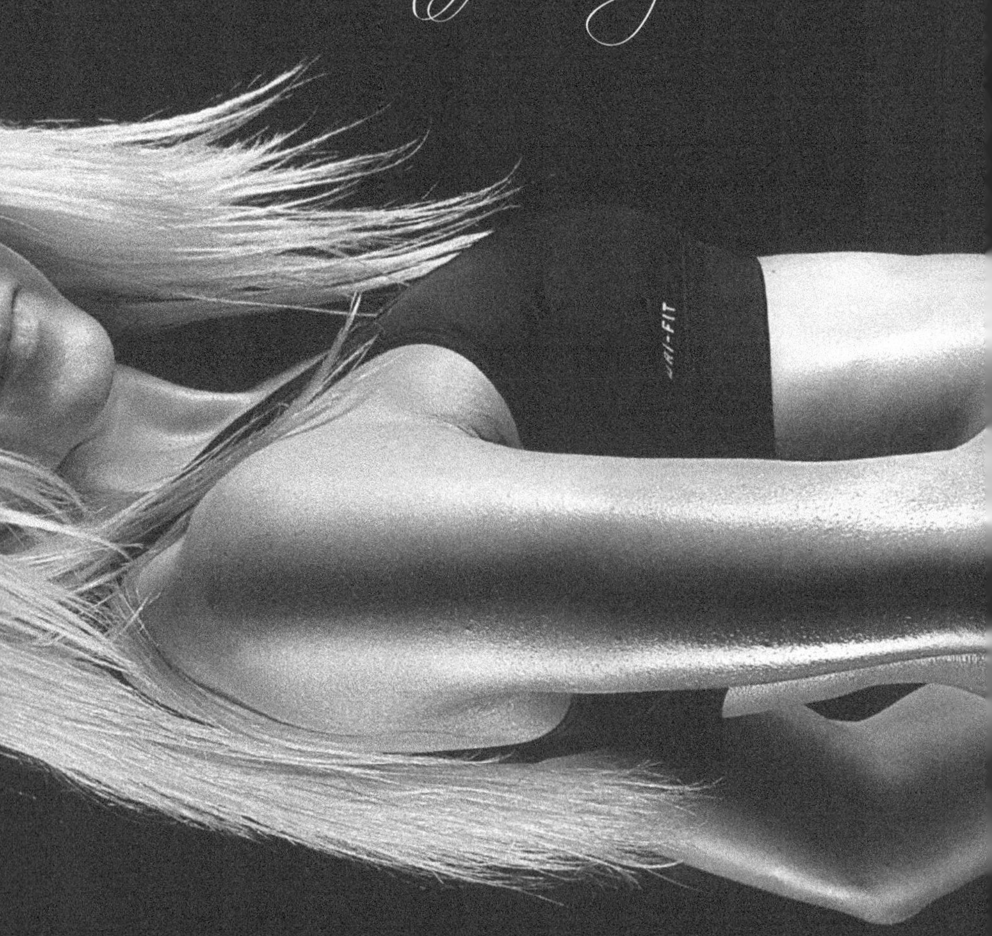

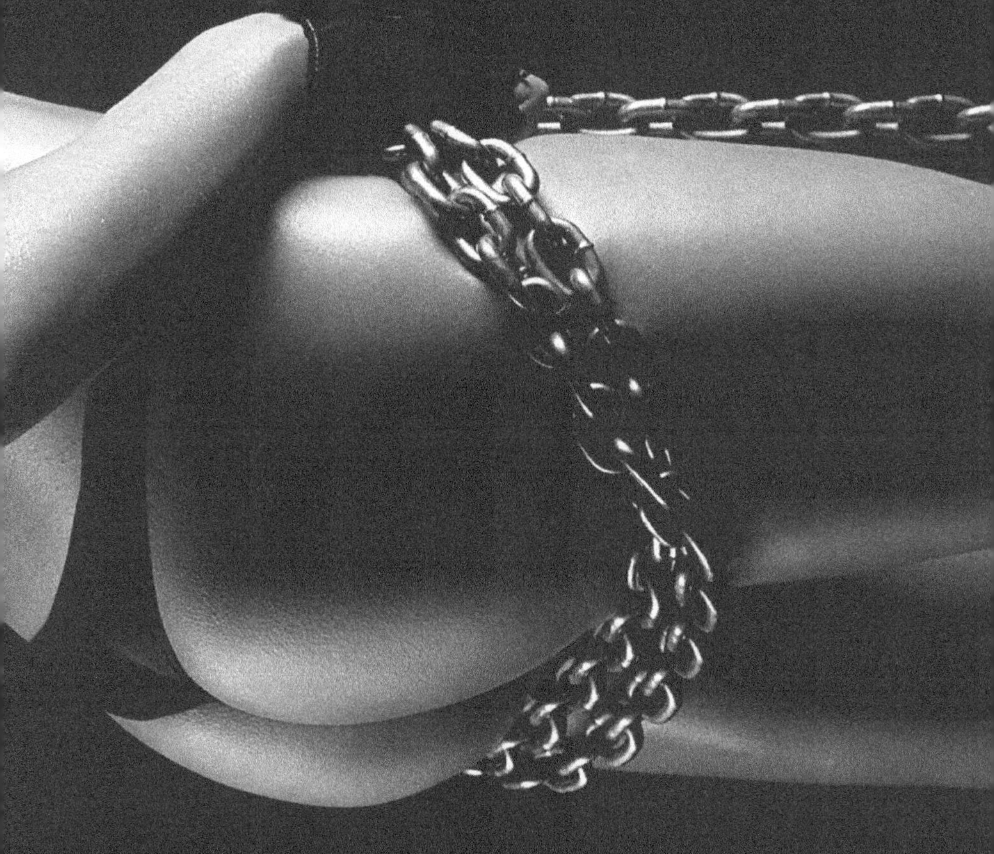

high ritual

The struggle for release is

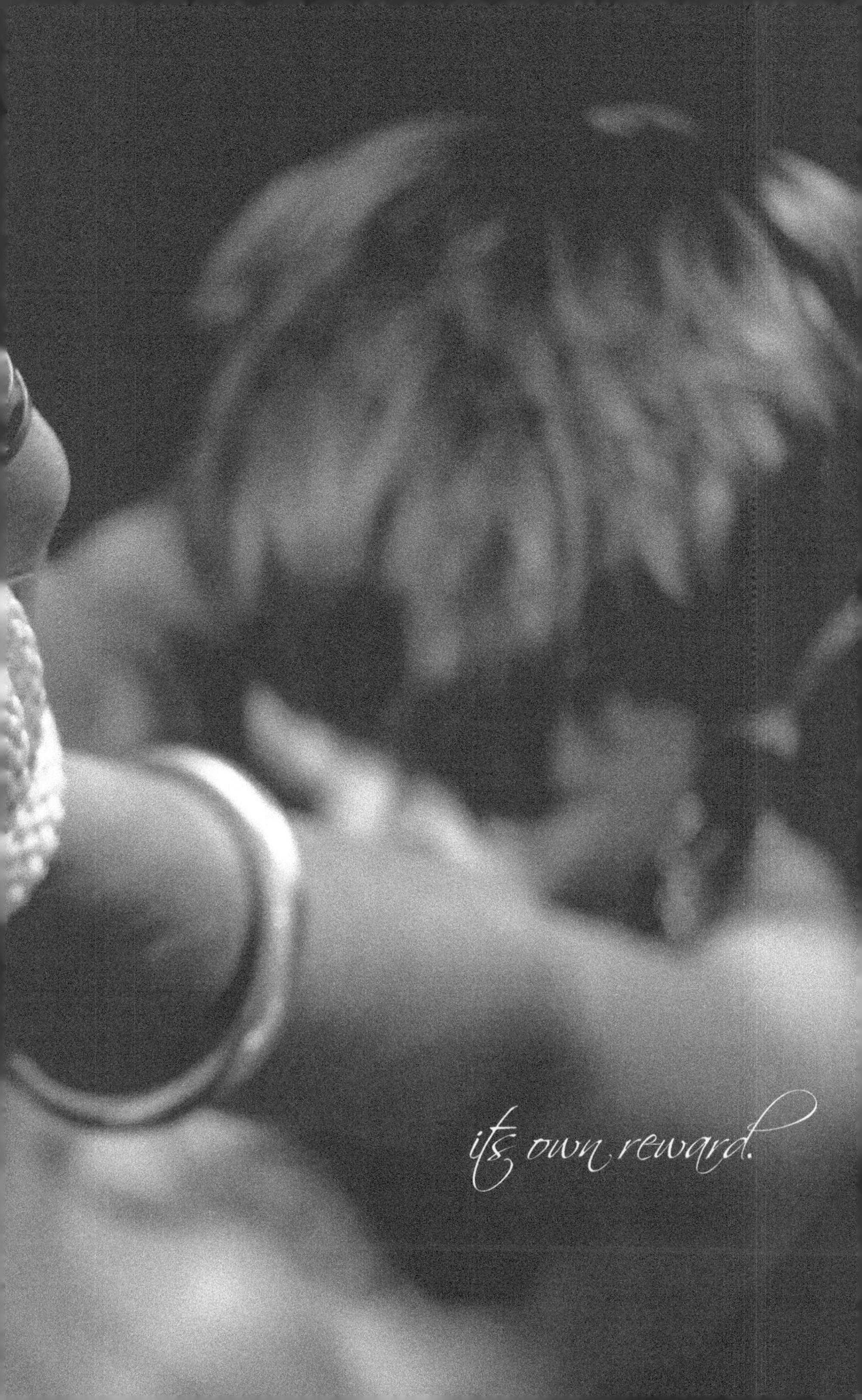

its own reward.

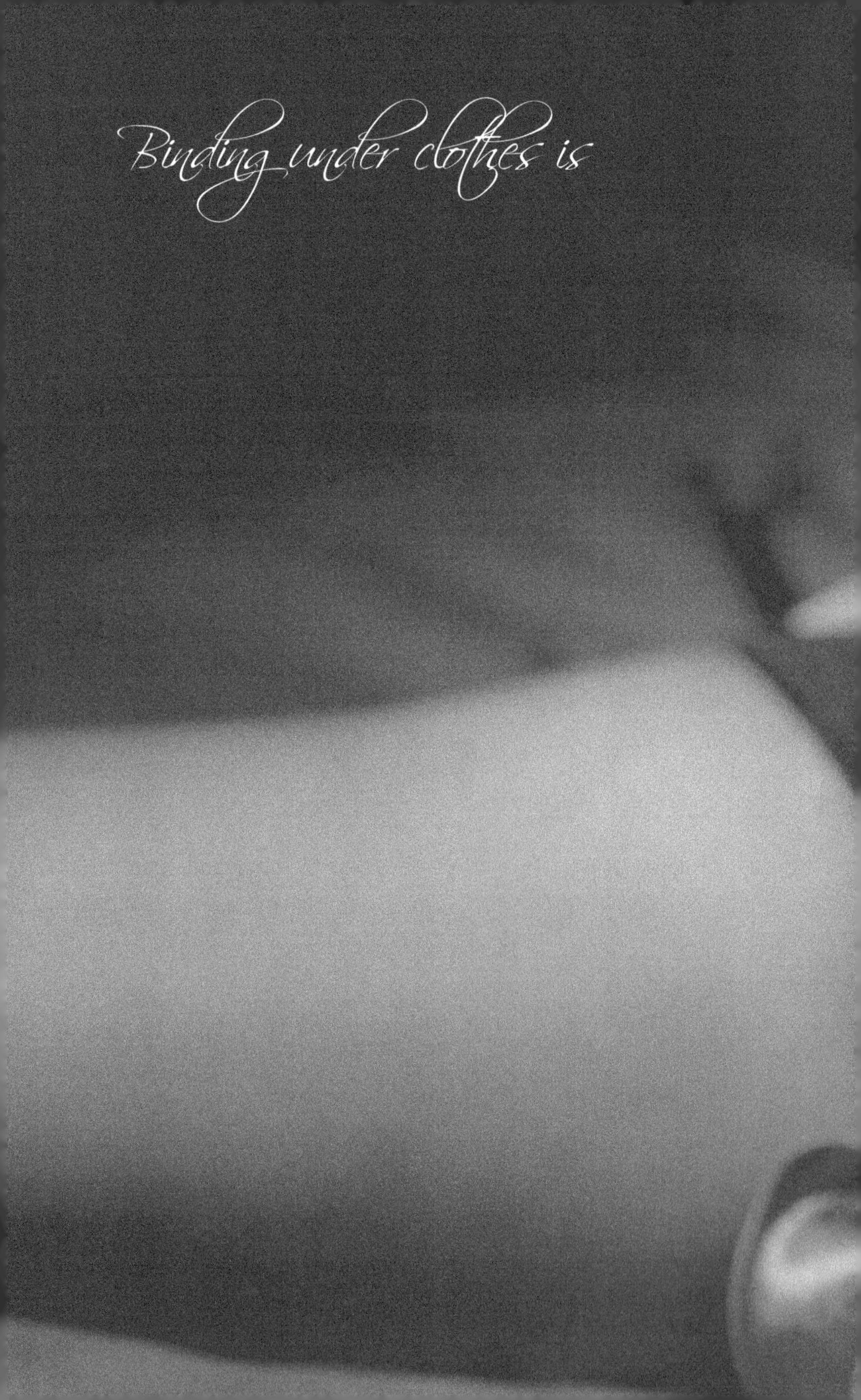

Binding under clothes is

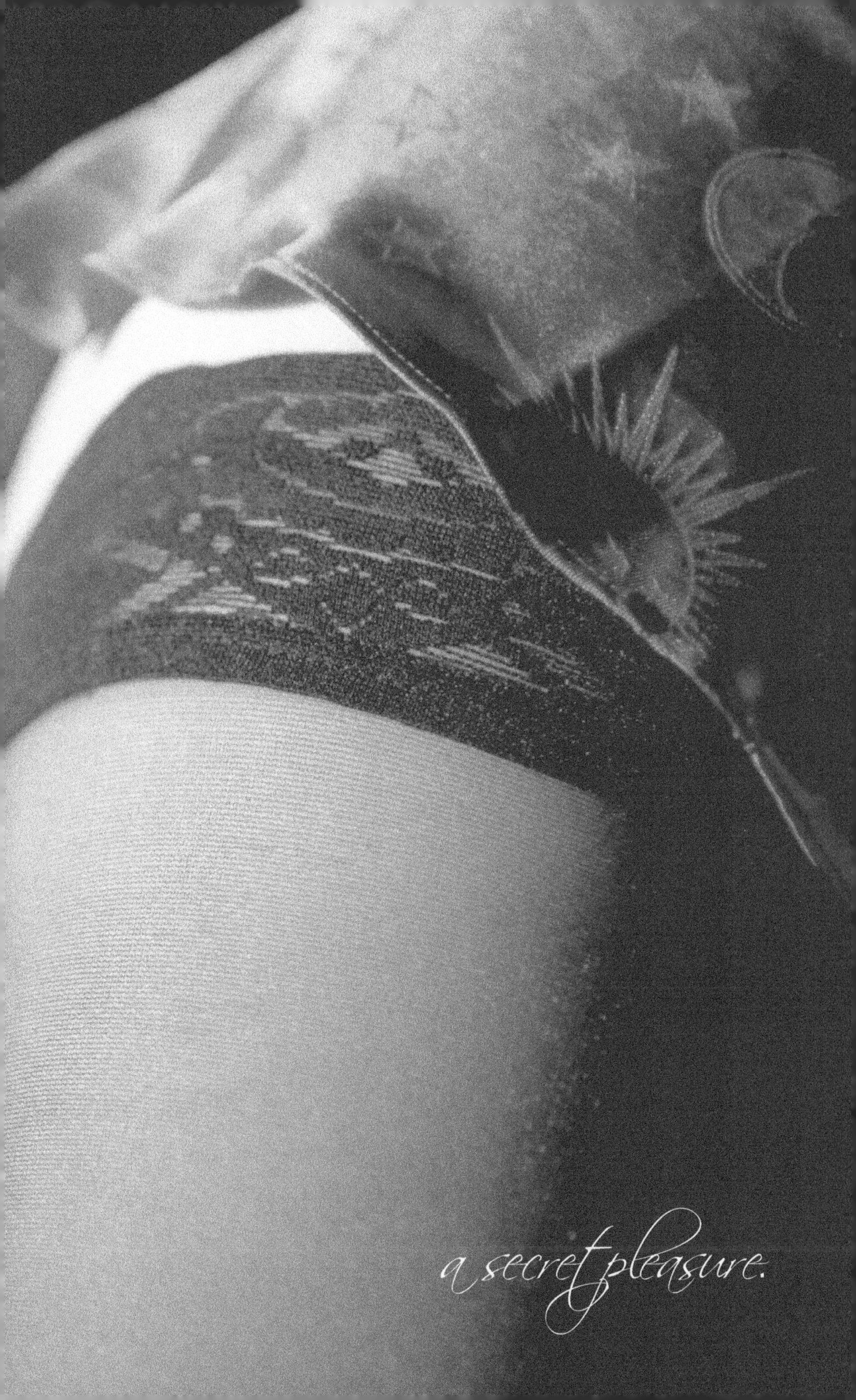

a secret pleasure.

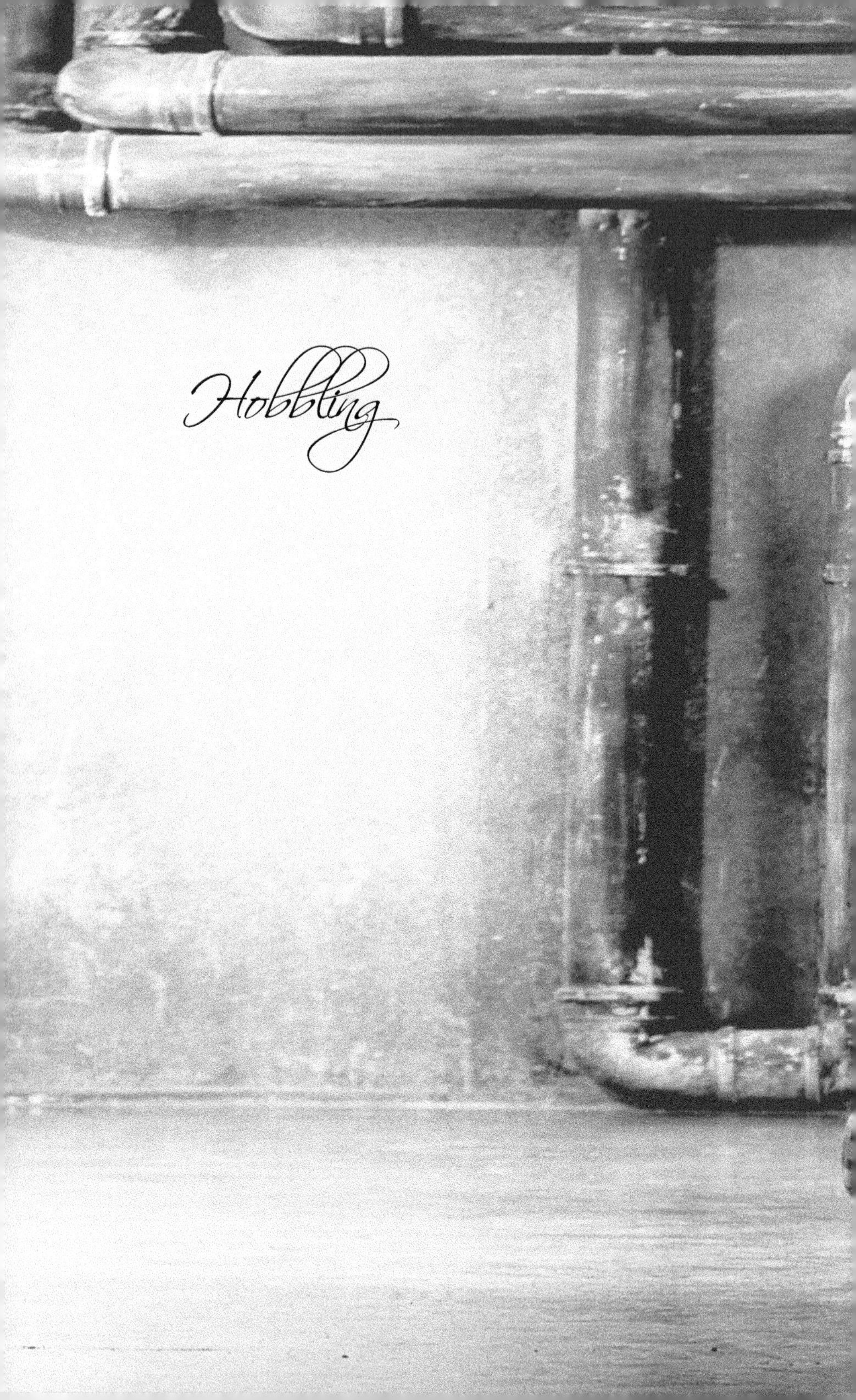

Hobbling

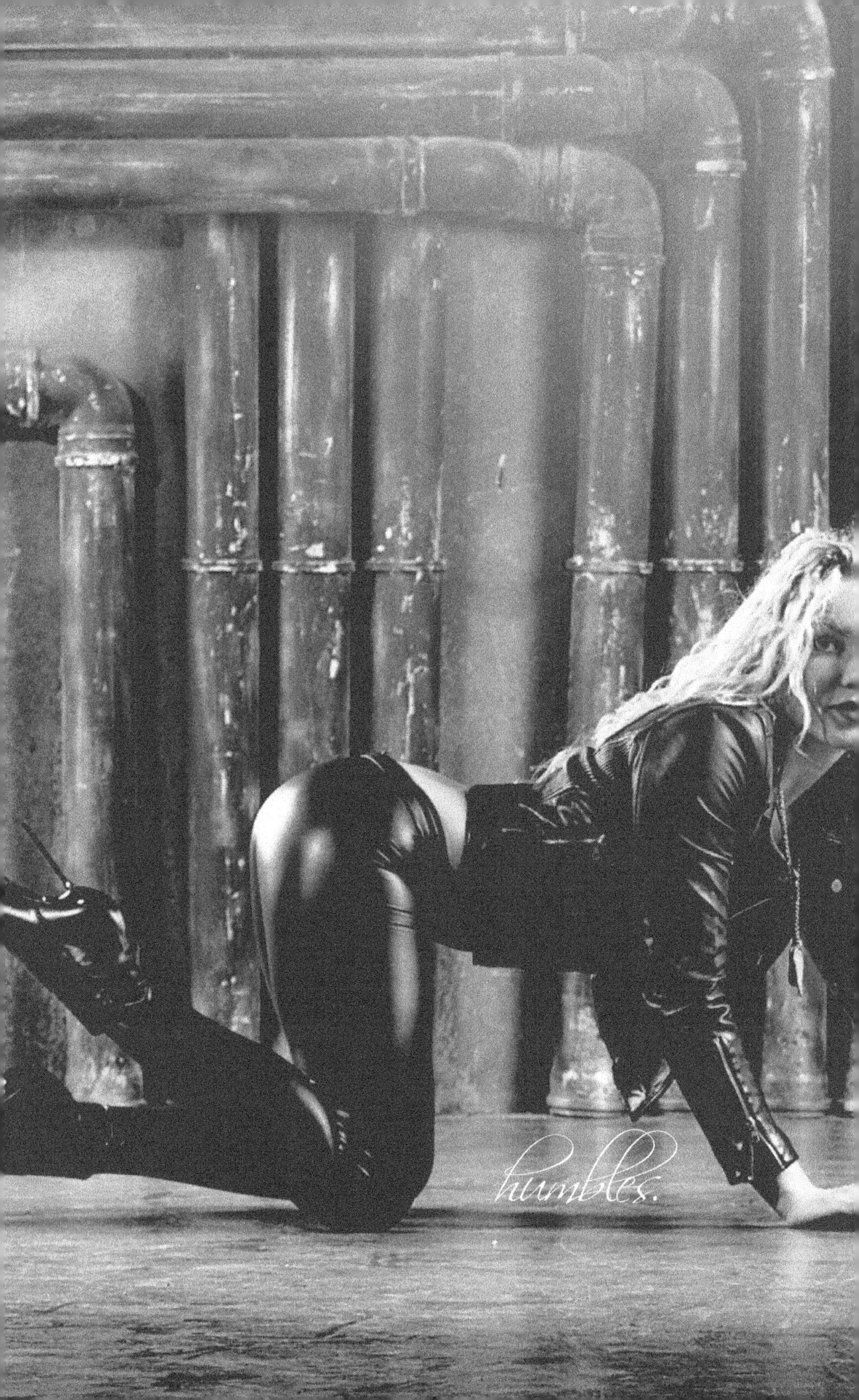
humbles.

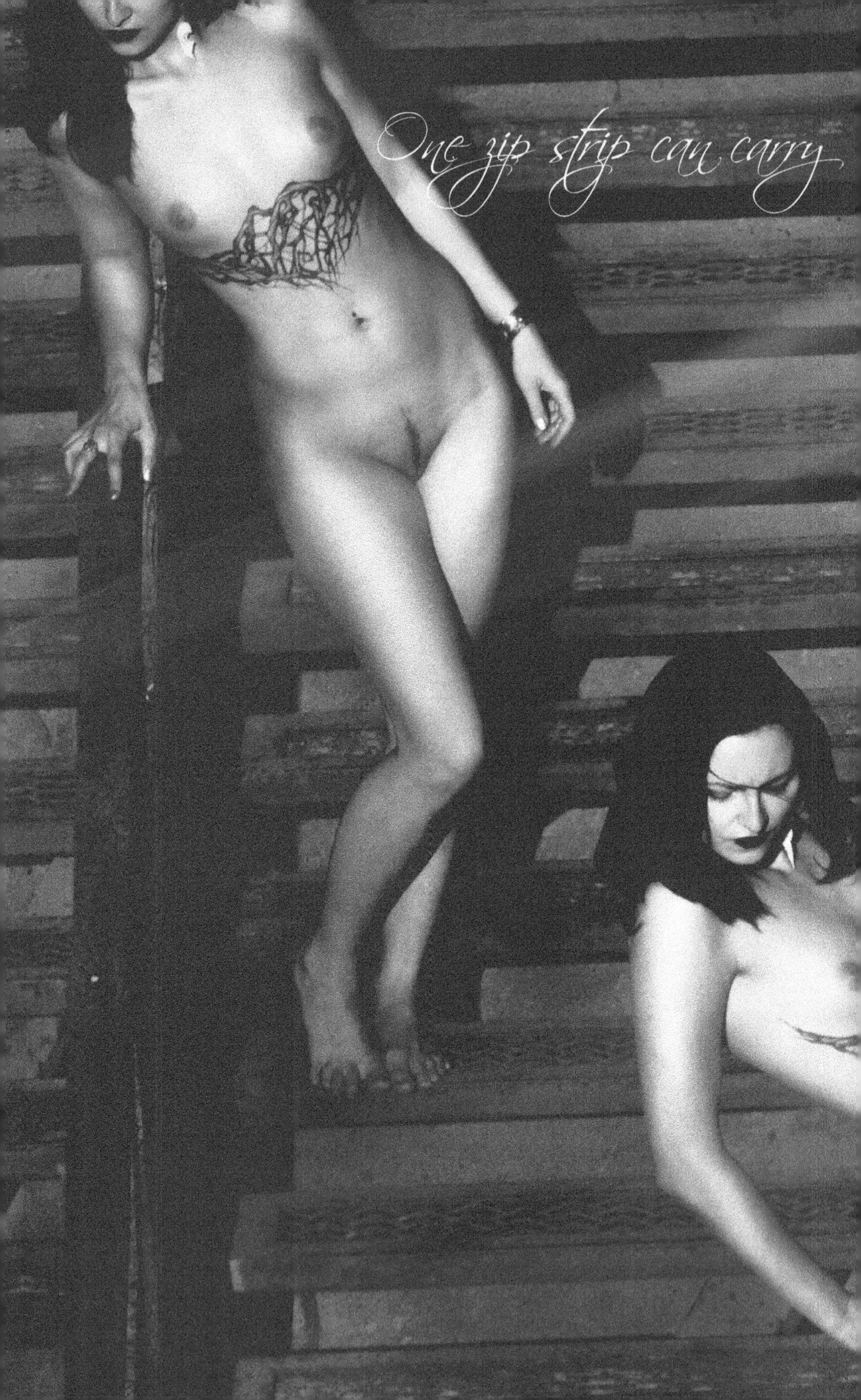
One zip strip can carry

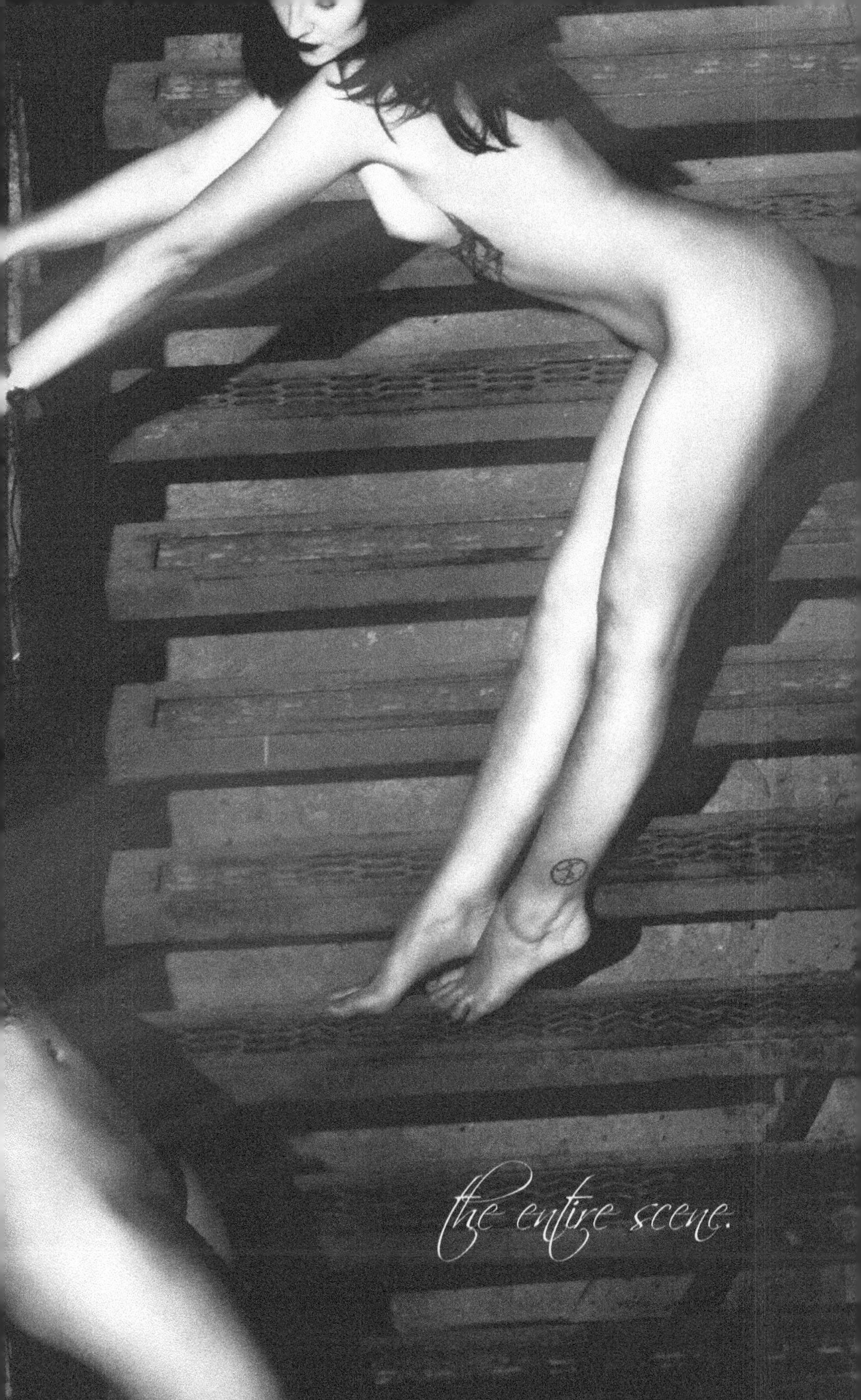
the entire scene.

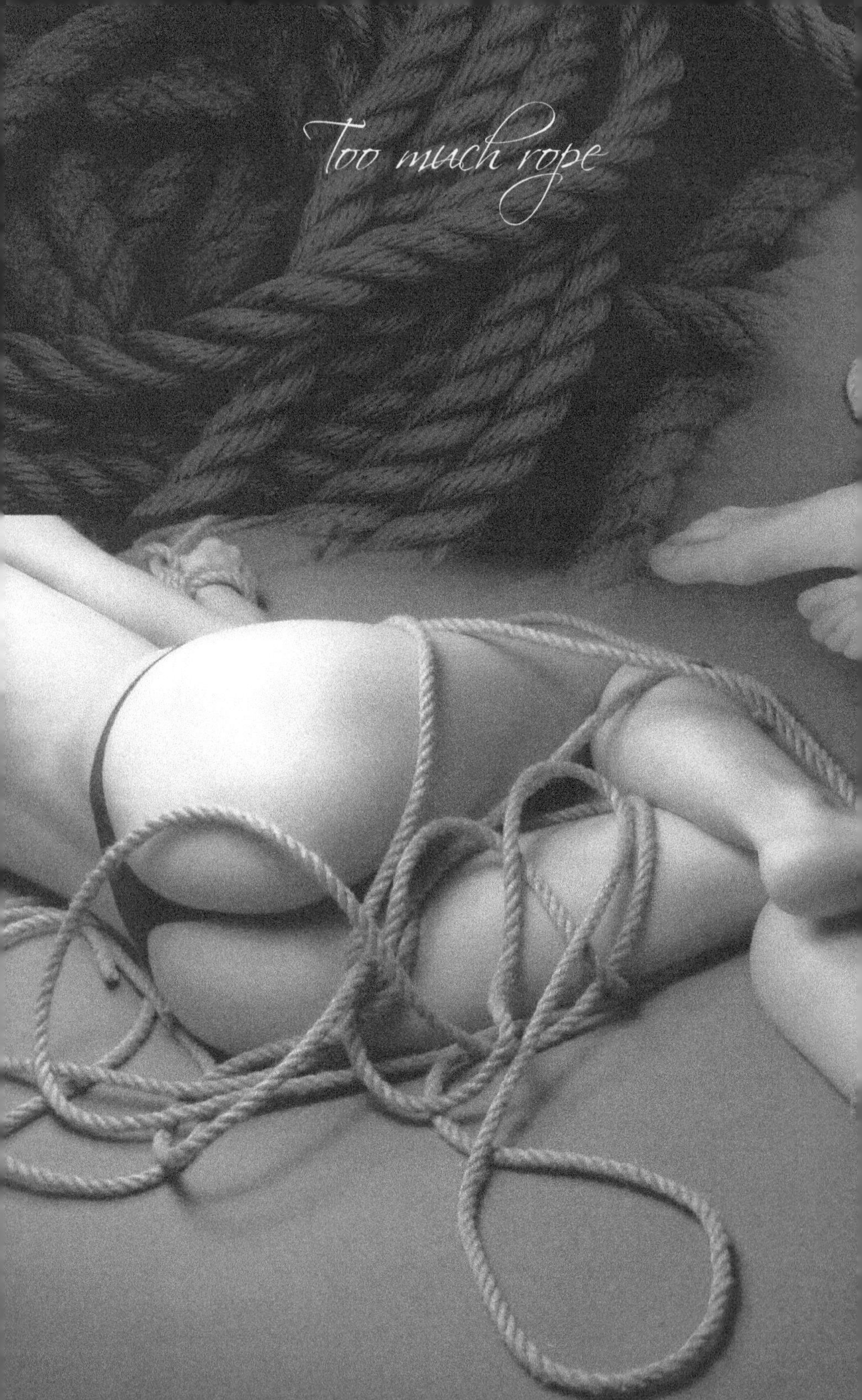
Too much rope

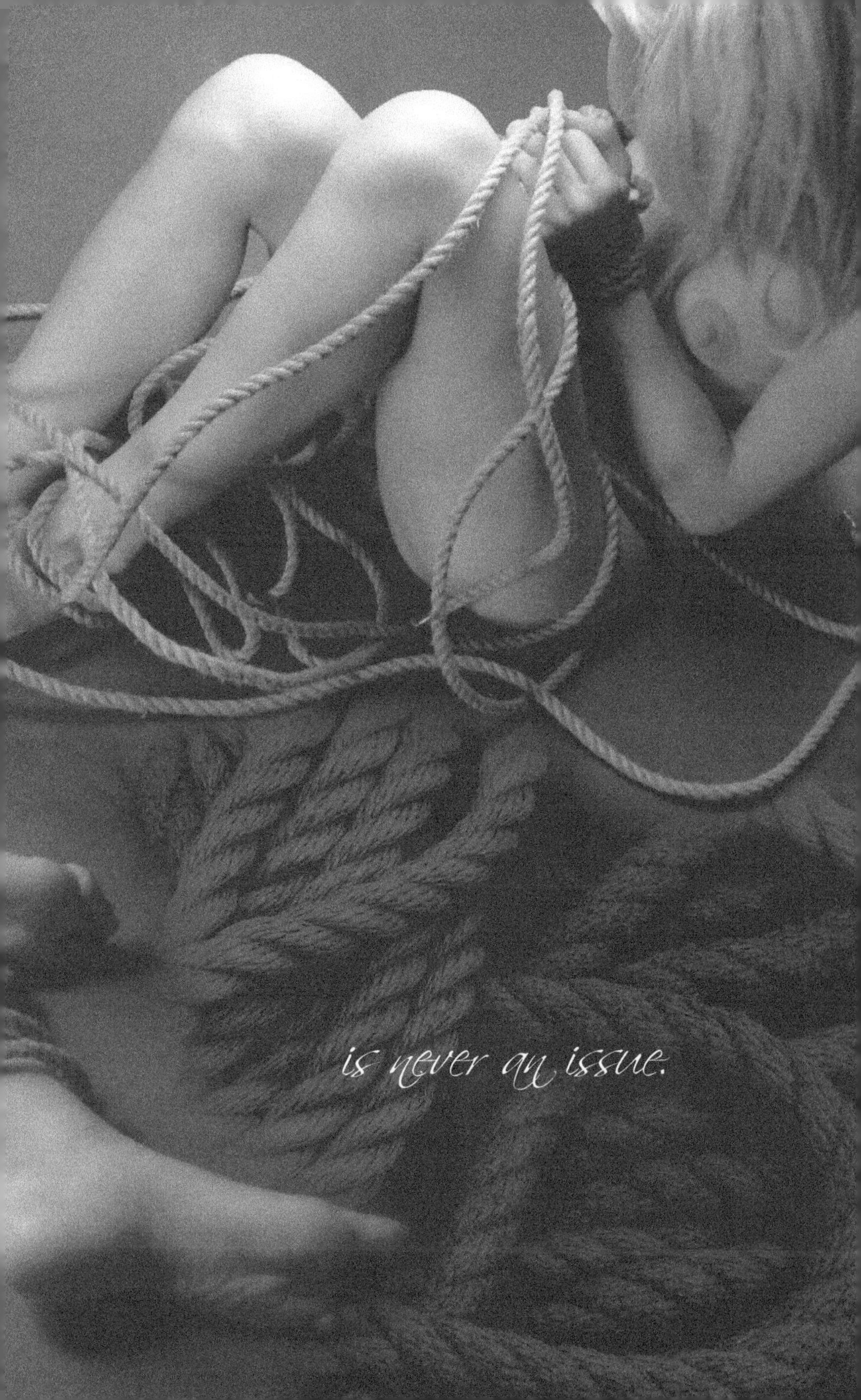
is never an issue.

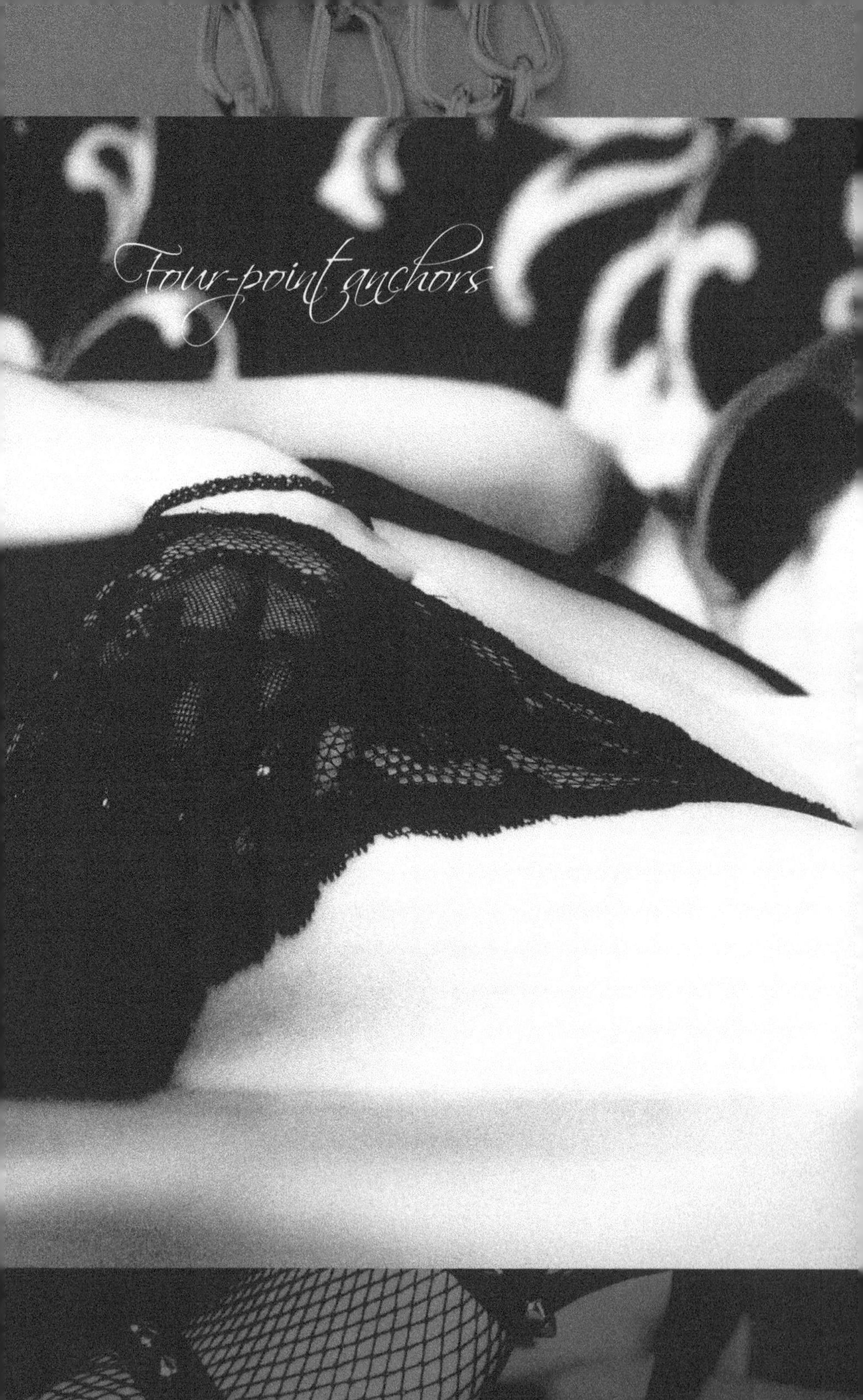
Four-point anchors

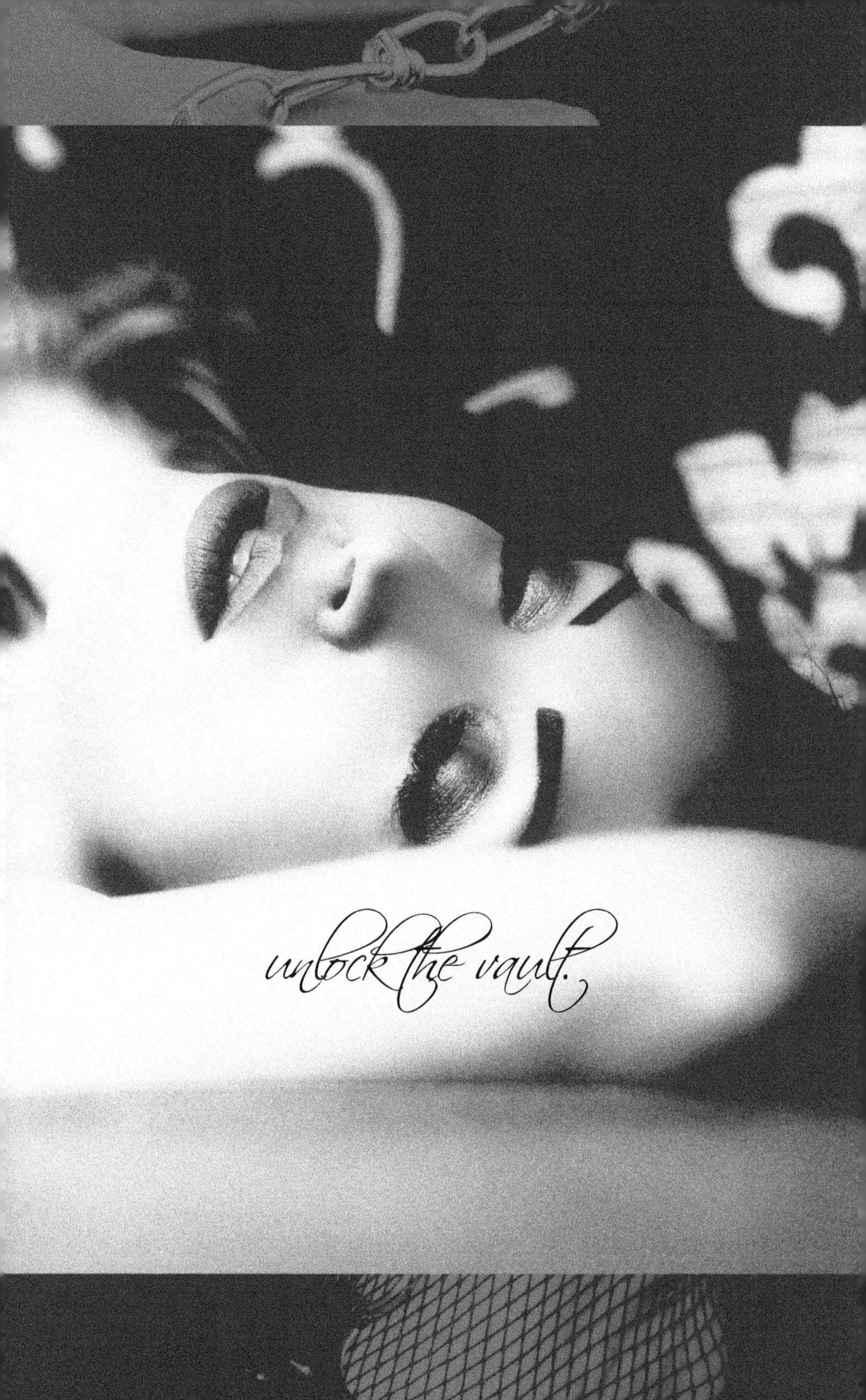
unlock the vault.

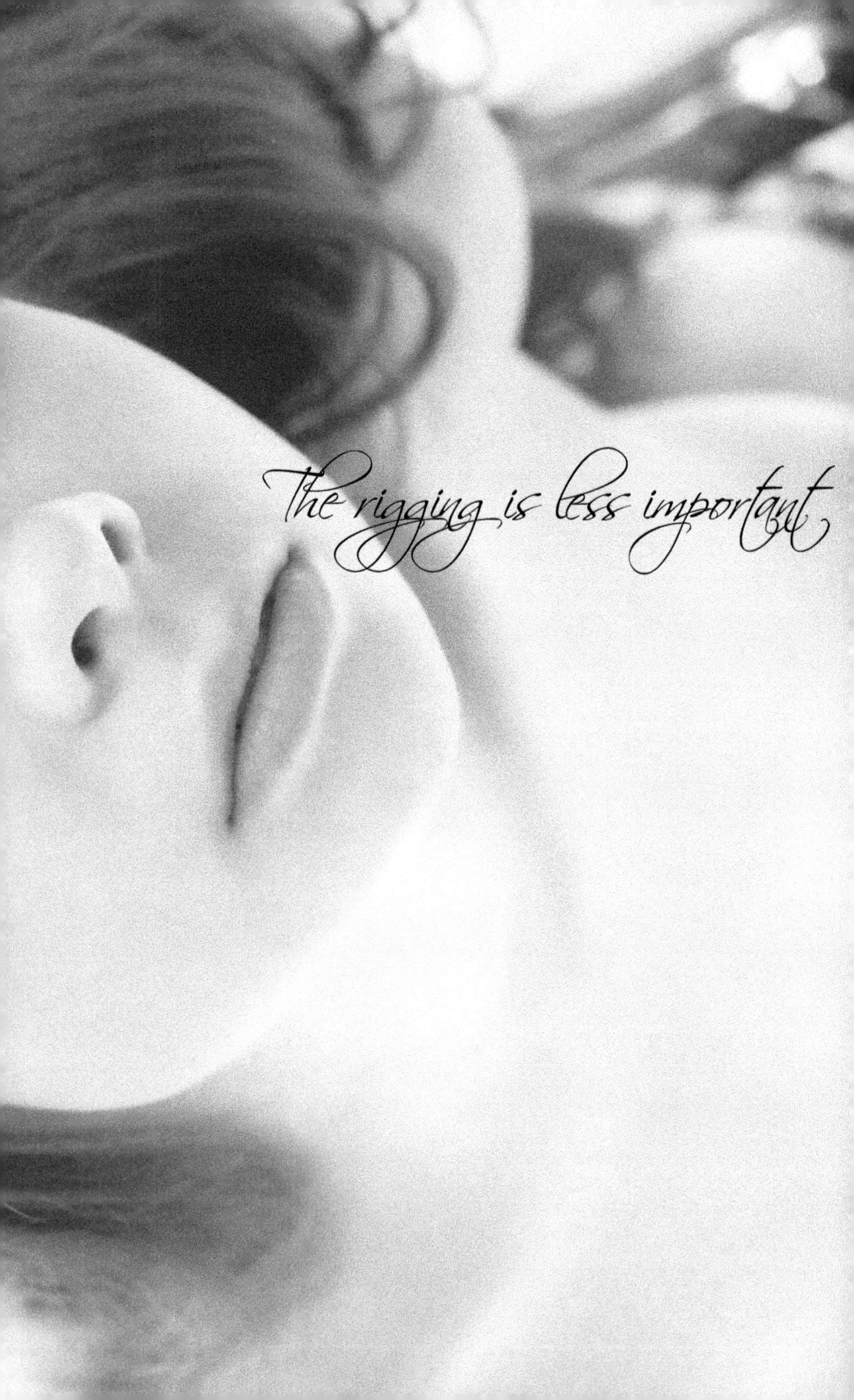

The rigging is less important

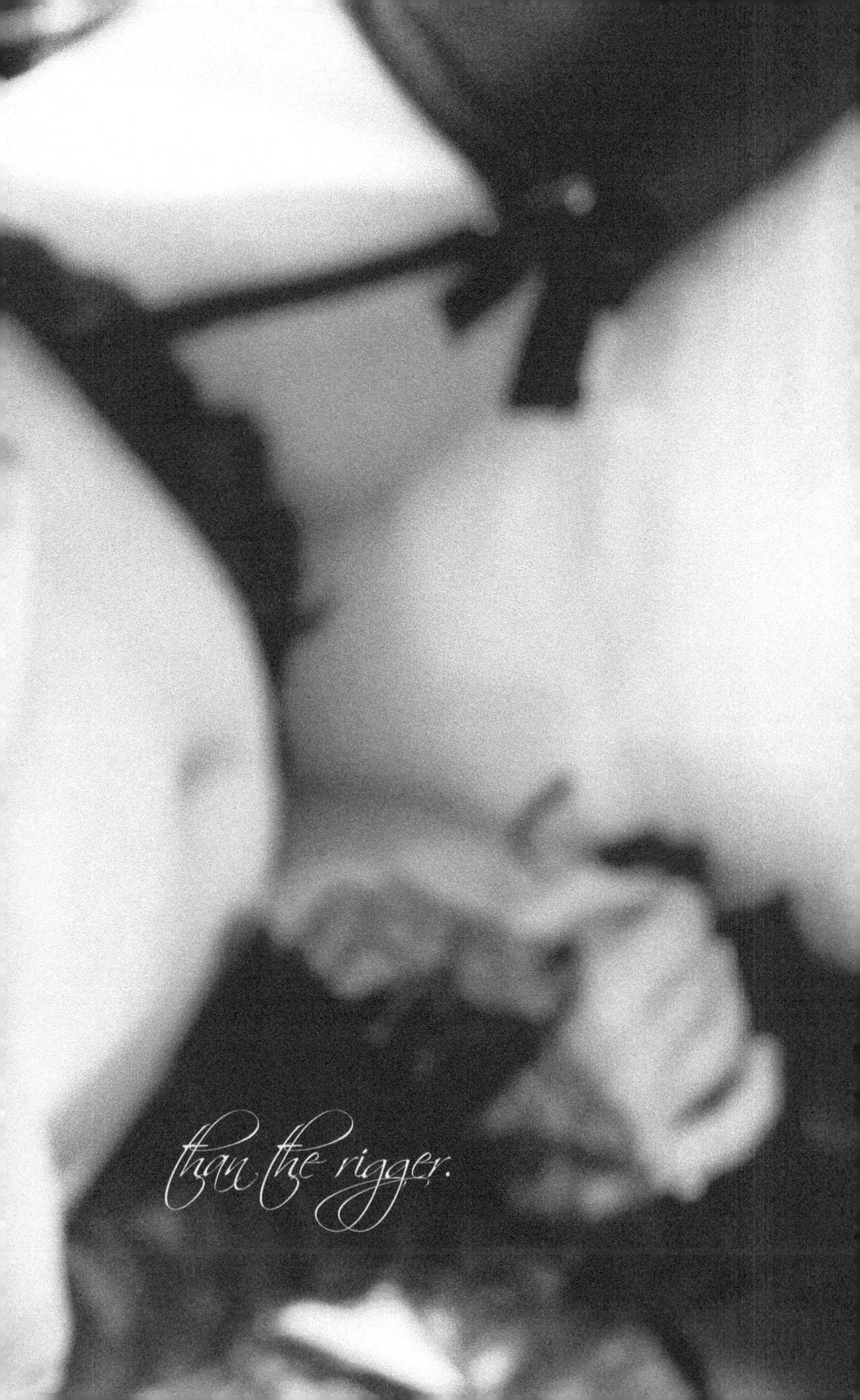

than the rigger.

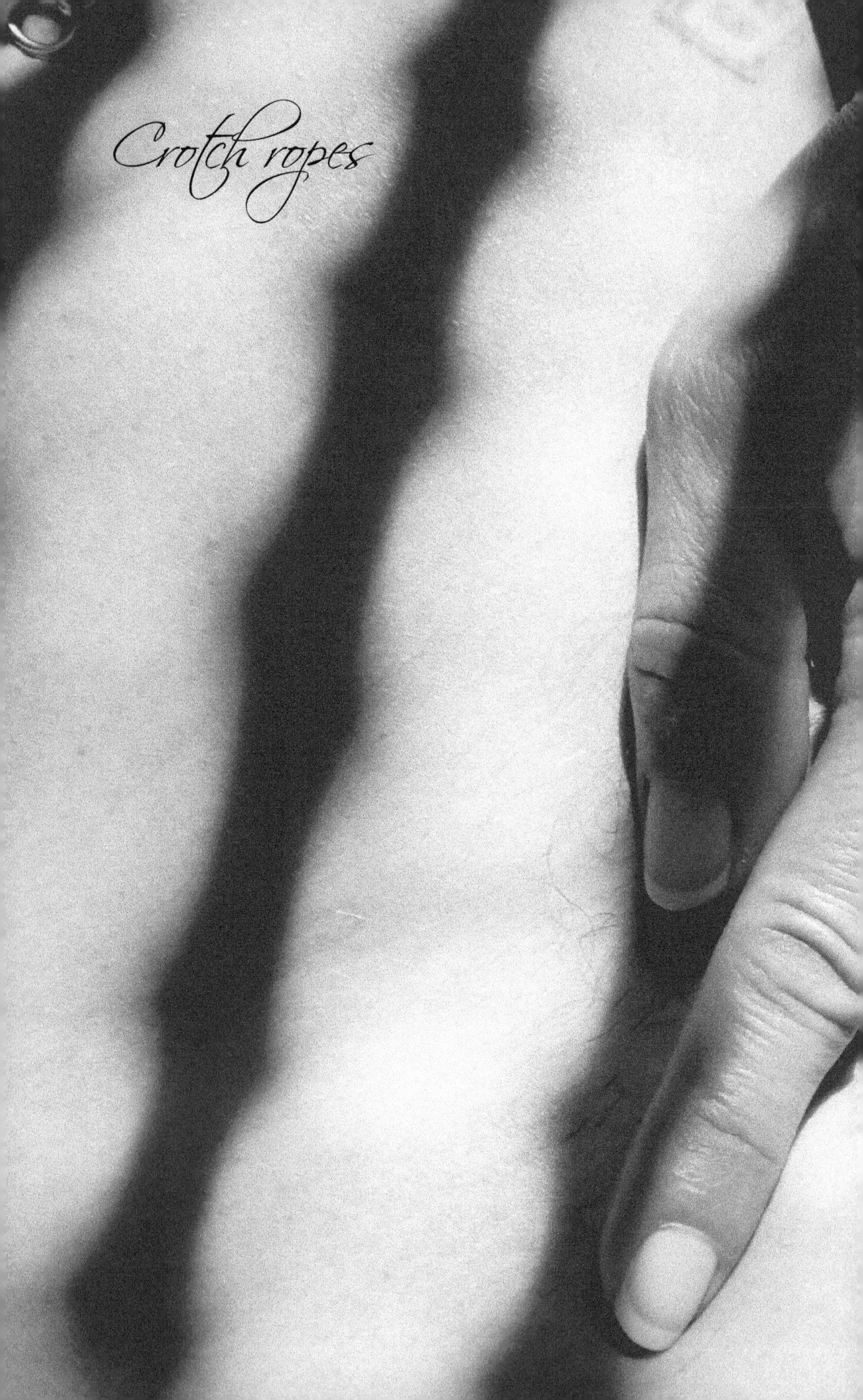
Crotch ropes

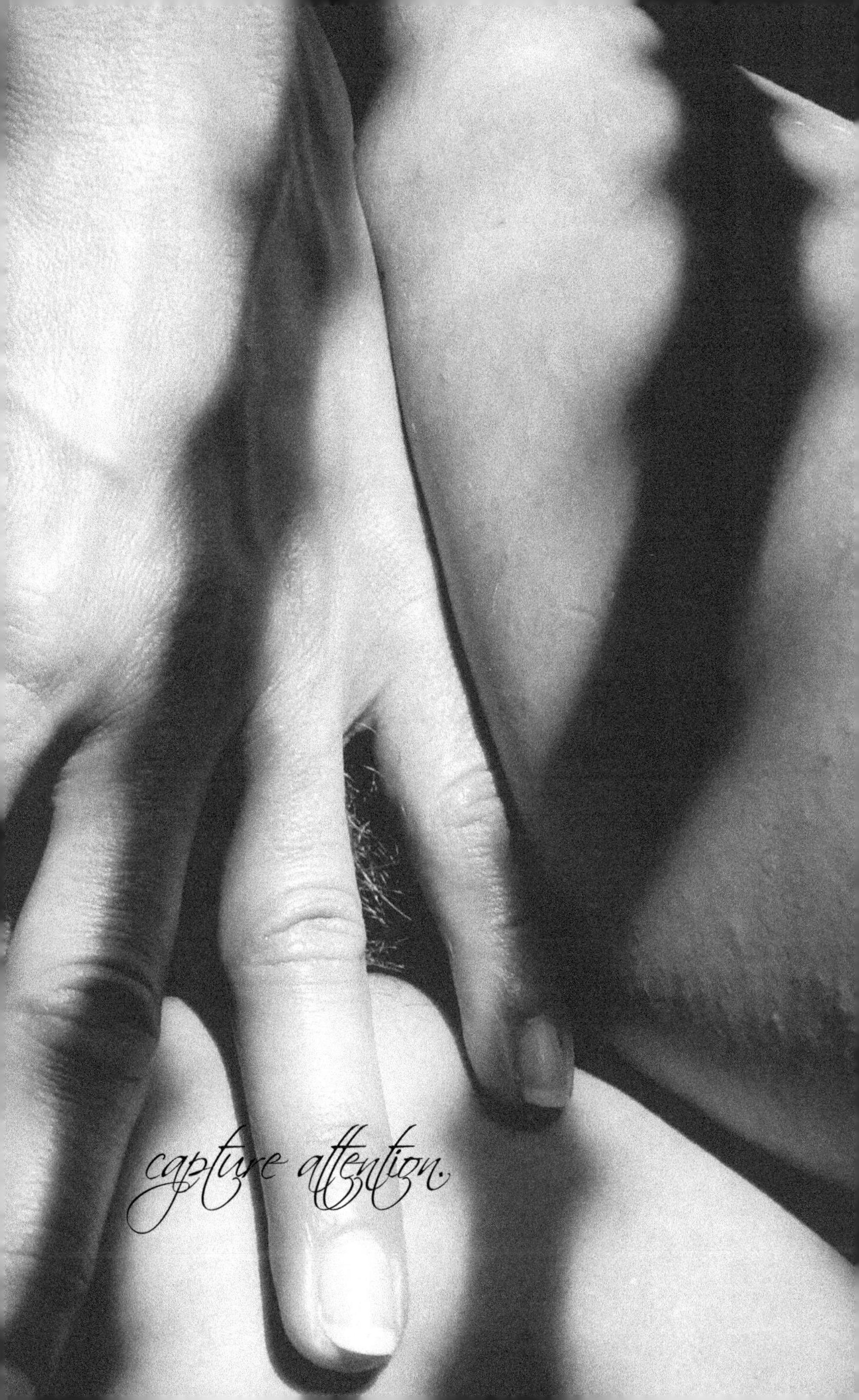

capture attention.

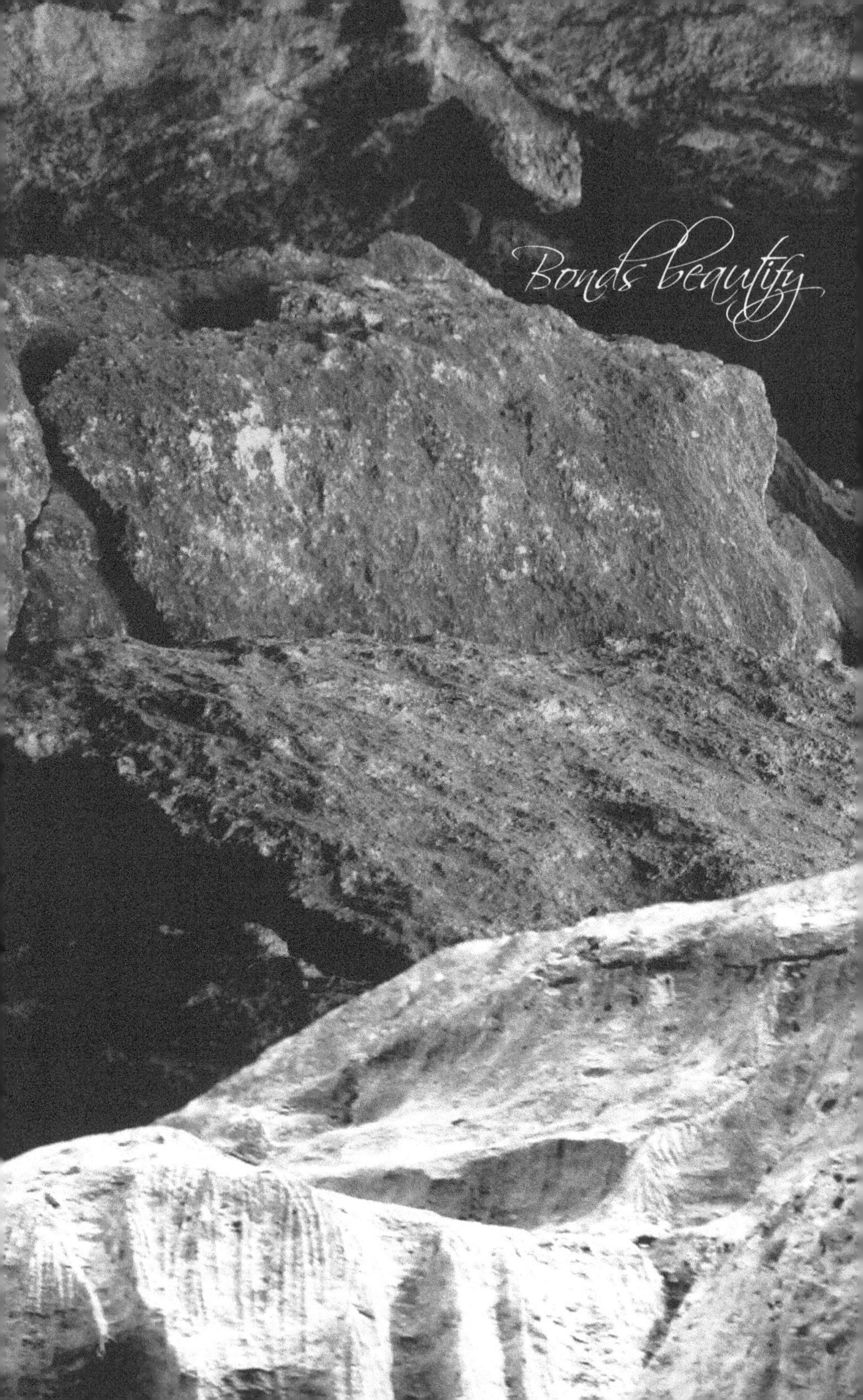
Bonds beautify

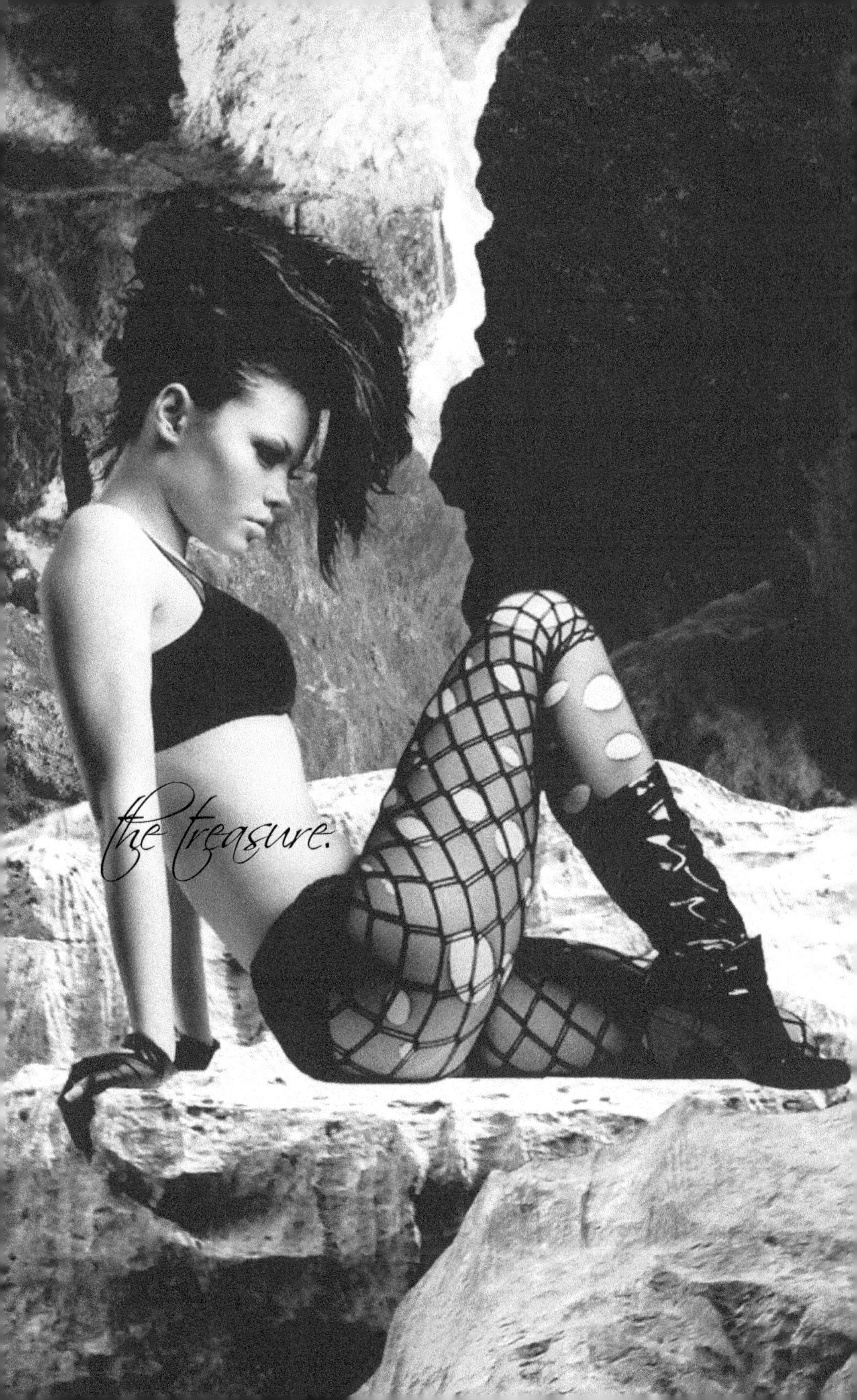
the treasure.

Total trust allows for

total vulnerability.

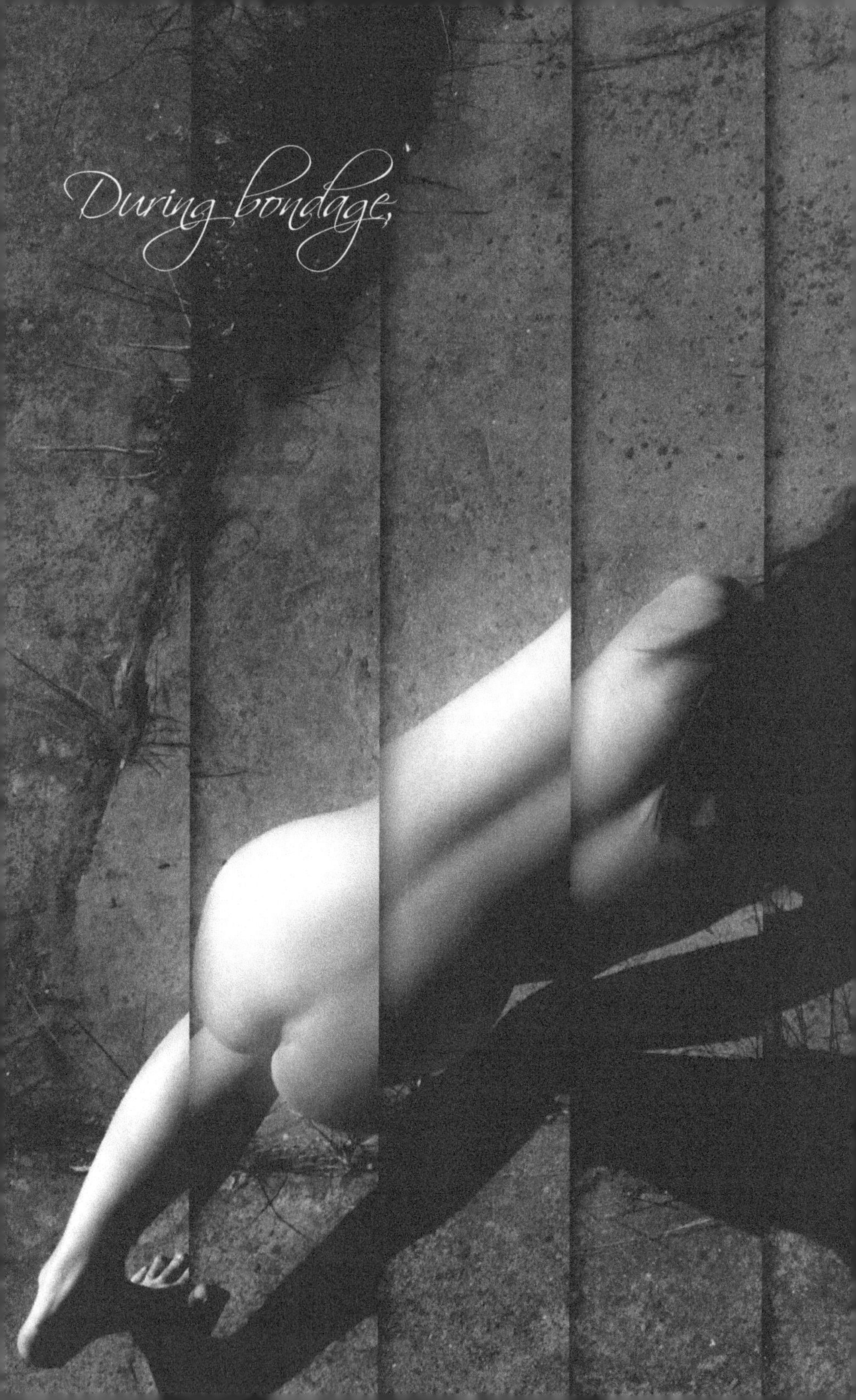
During bondage,

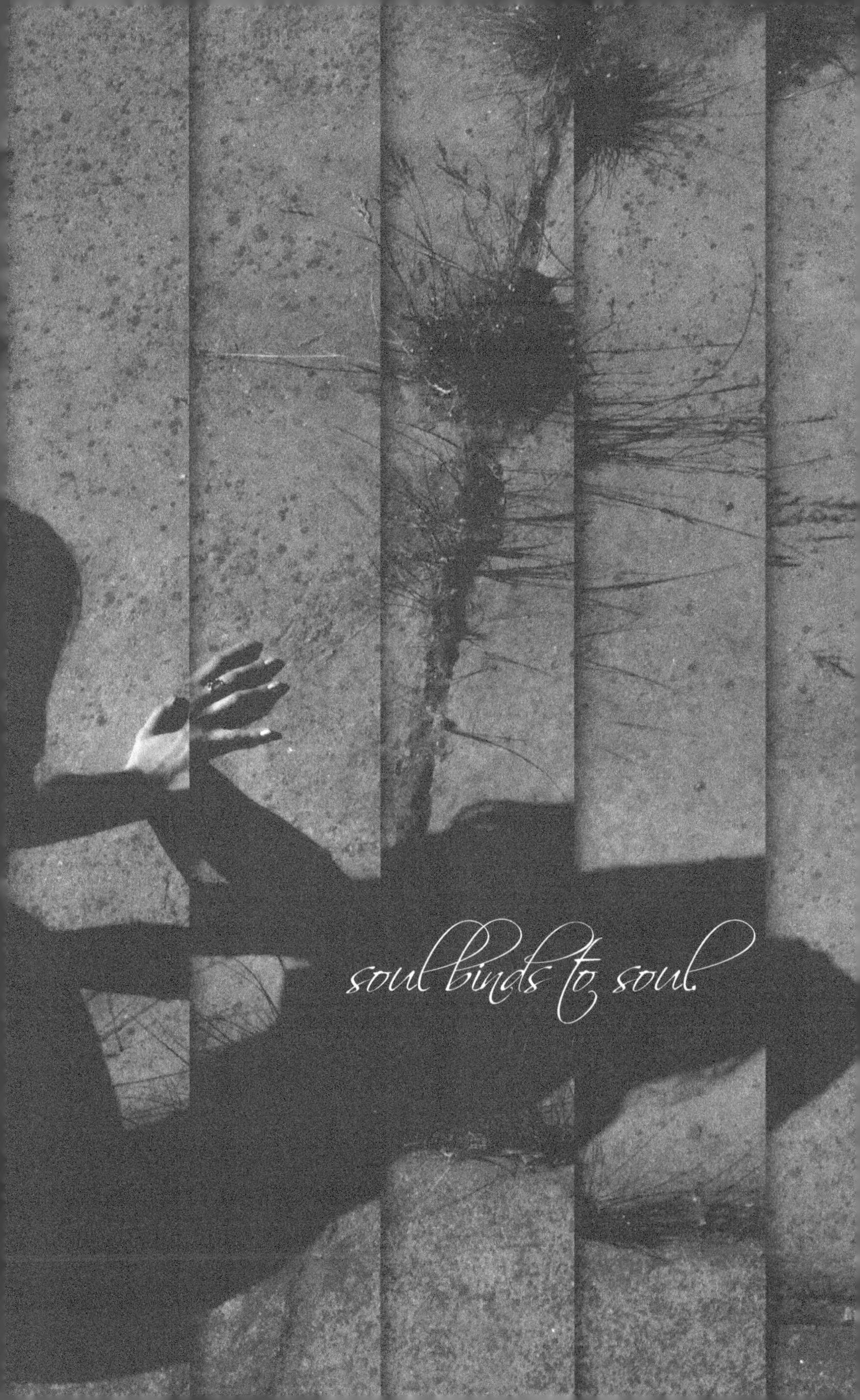

soul binds to soul.

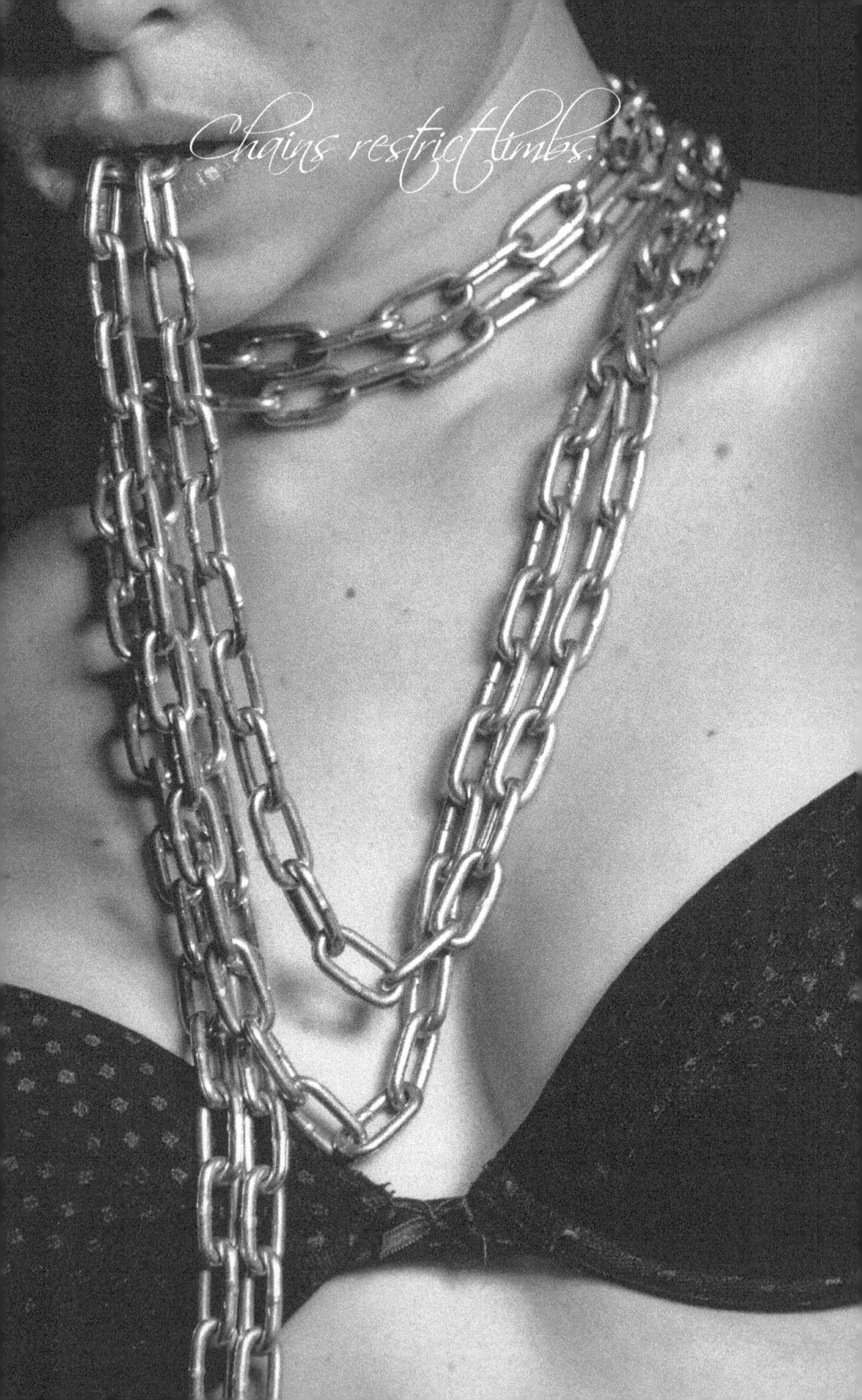
Chains restrict limbs.

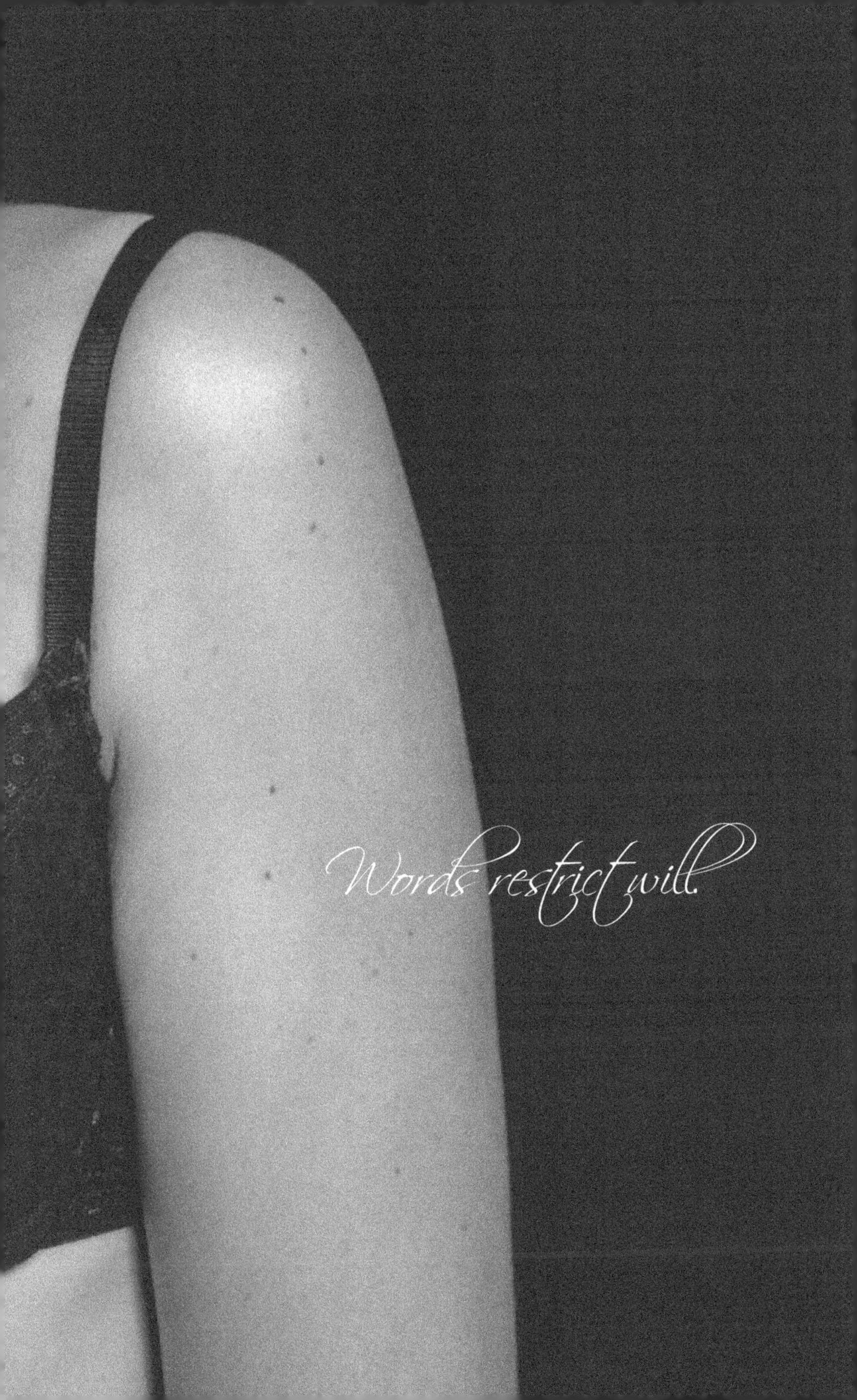

Words restrict will.

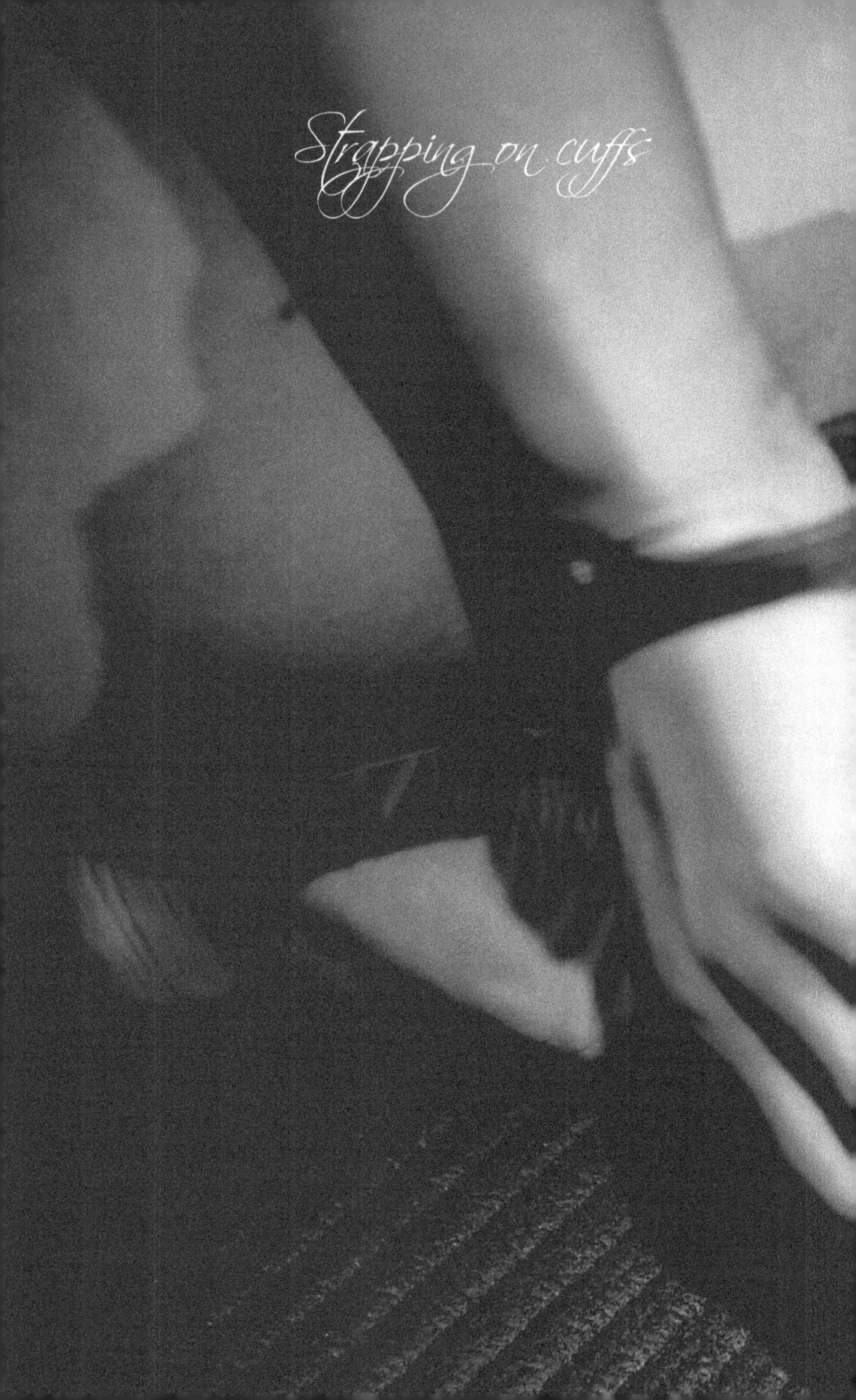

Strapping on cuffs

strips away defenses.

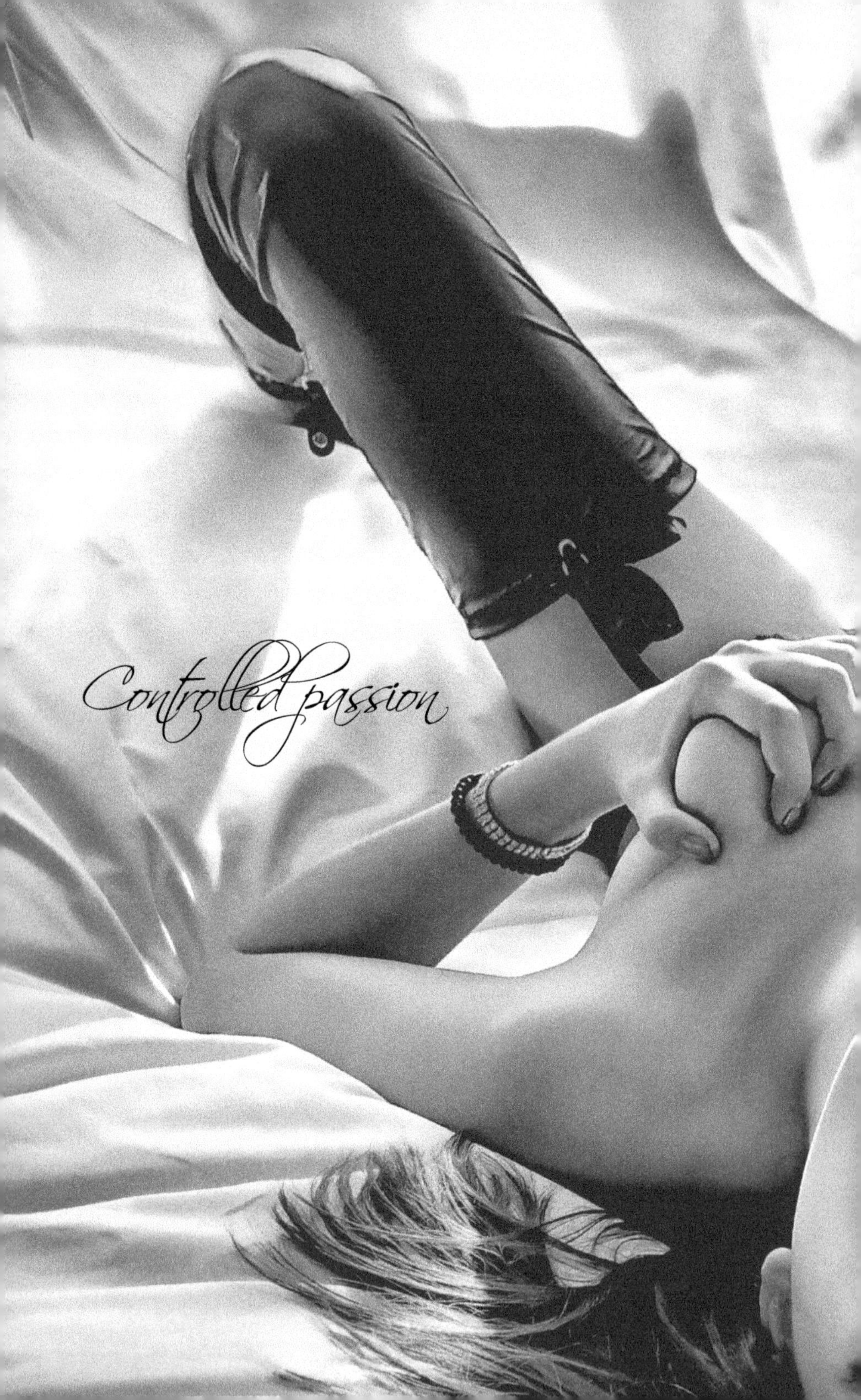
Controlled passion

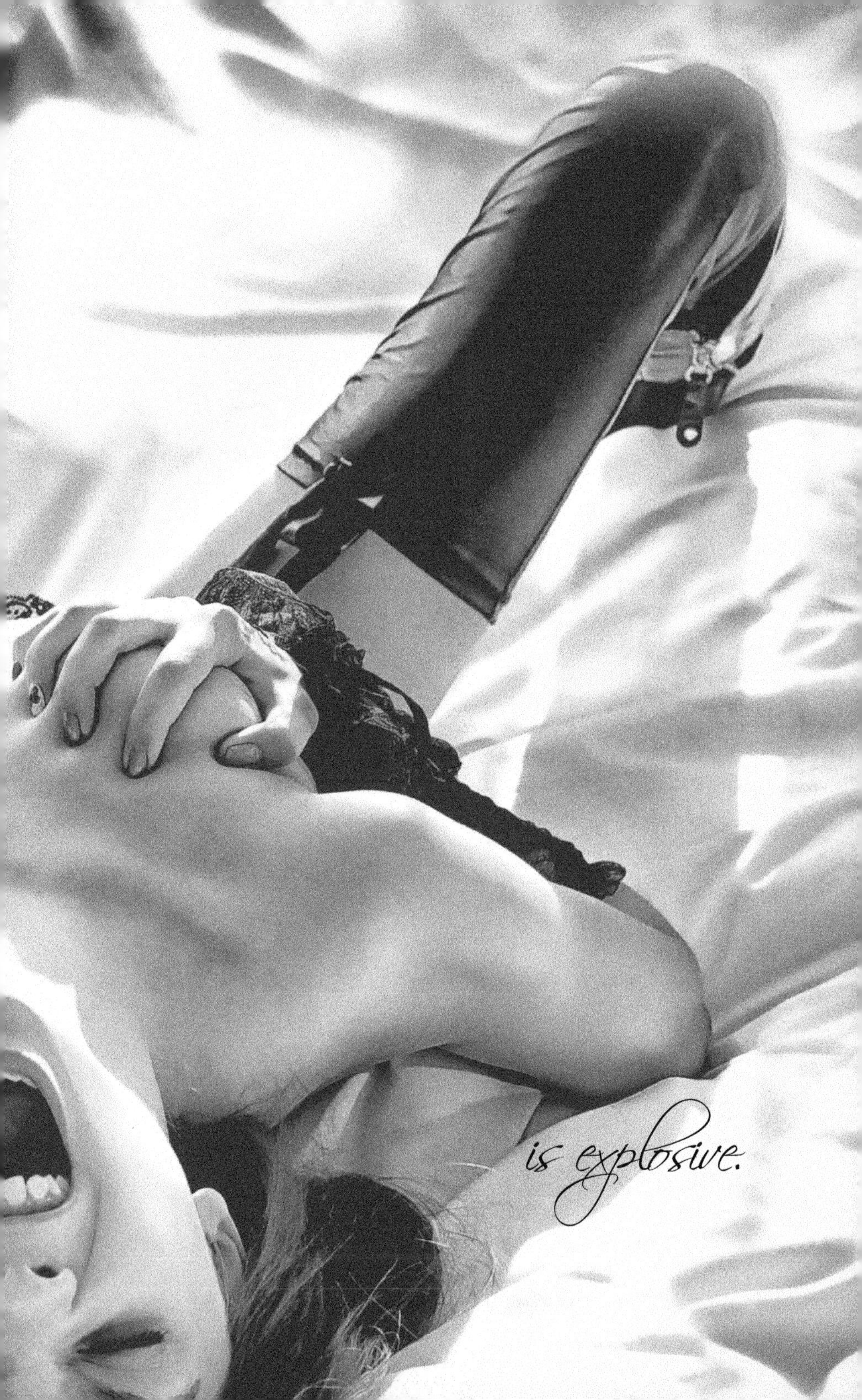
is explosive.

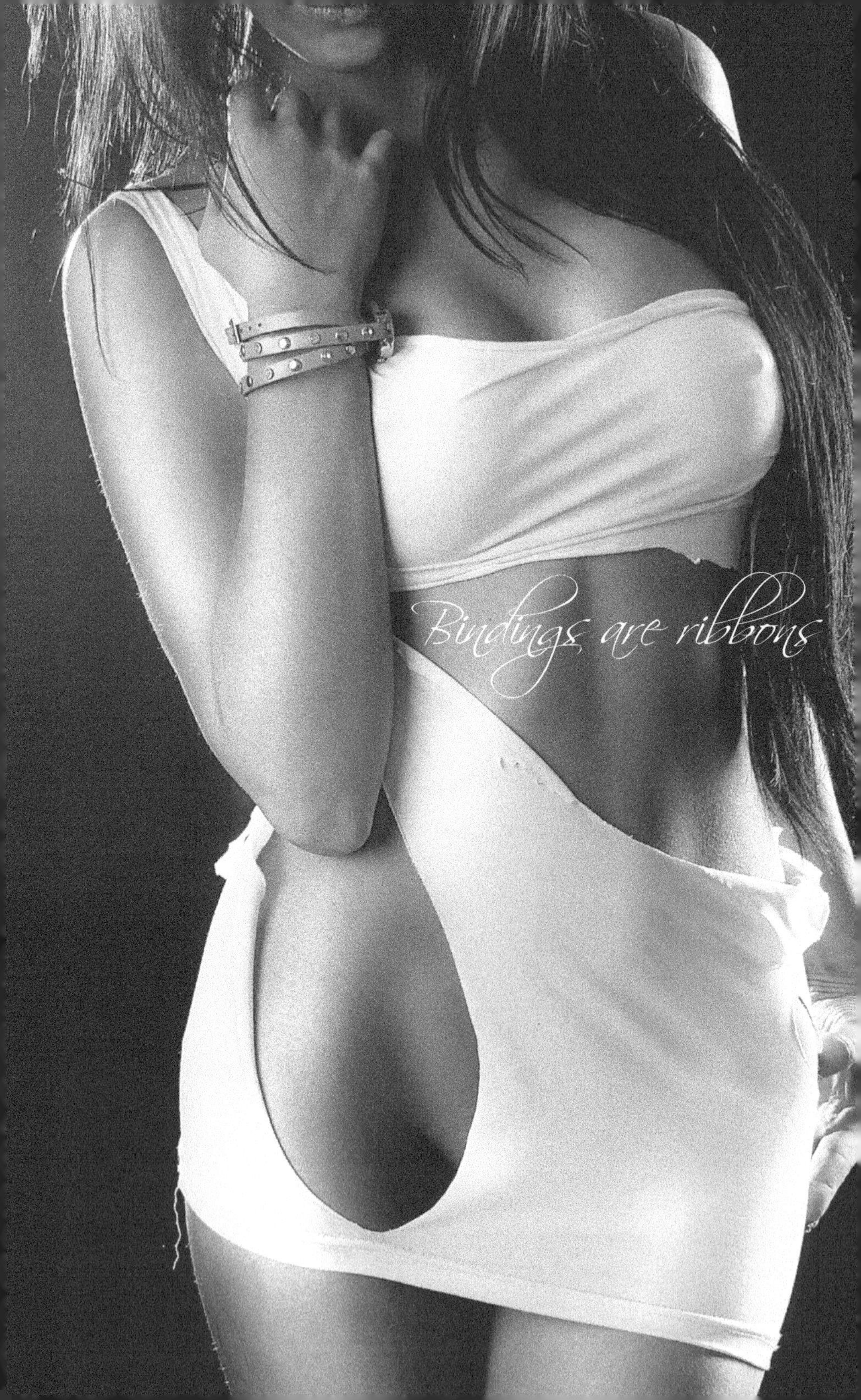

Bindings are ribbons

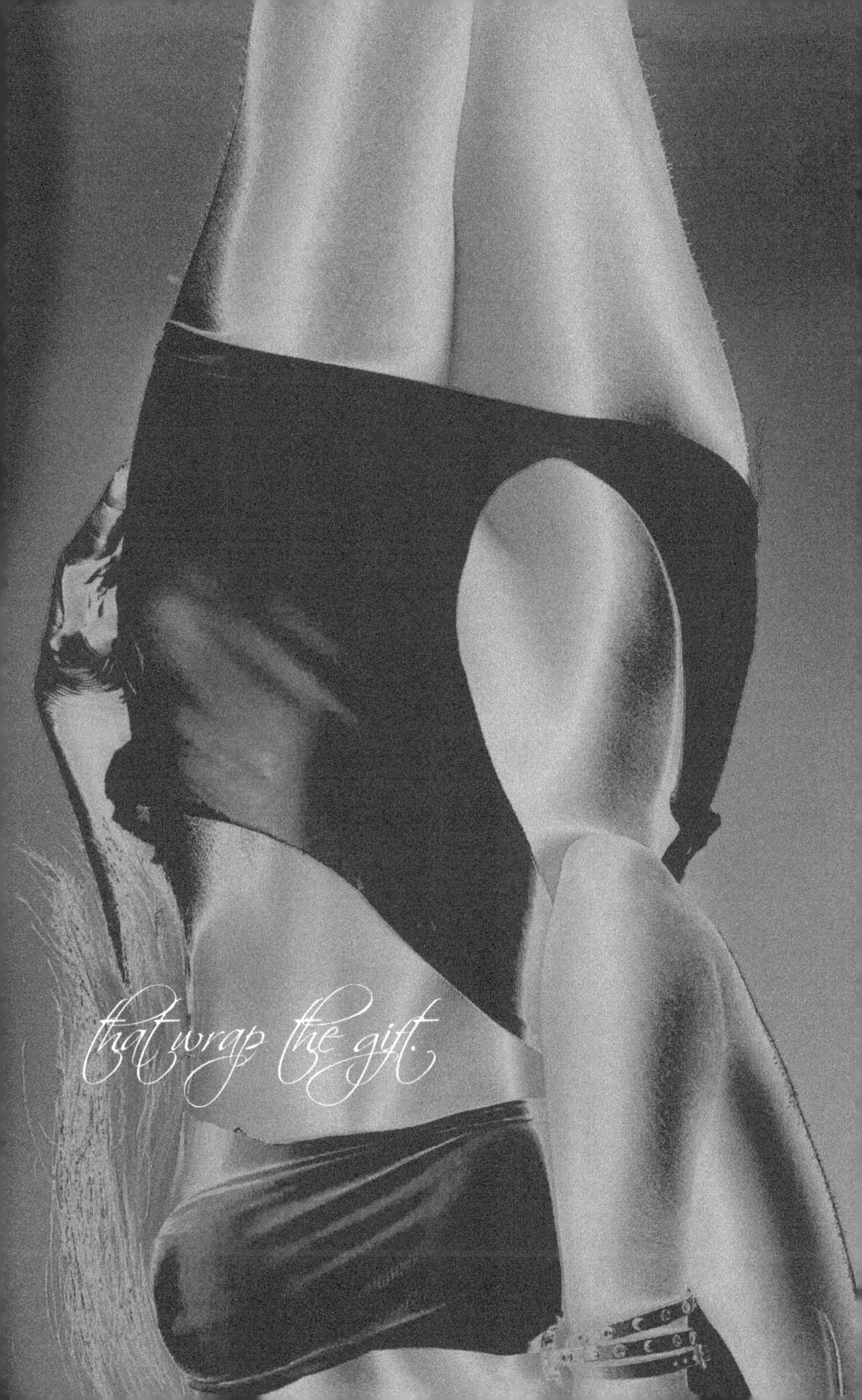

that wrap the gift.

Breast bondage

highlights beauty.

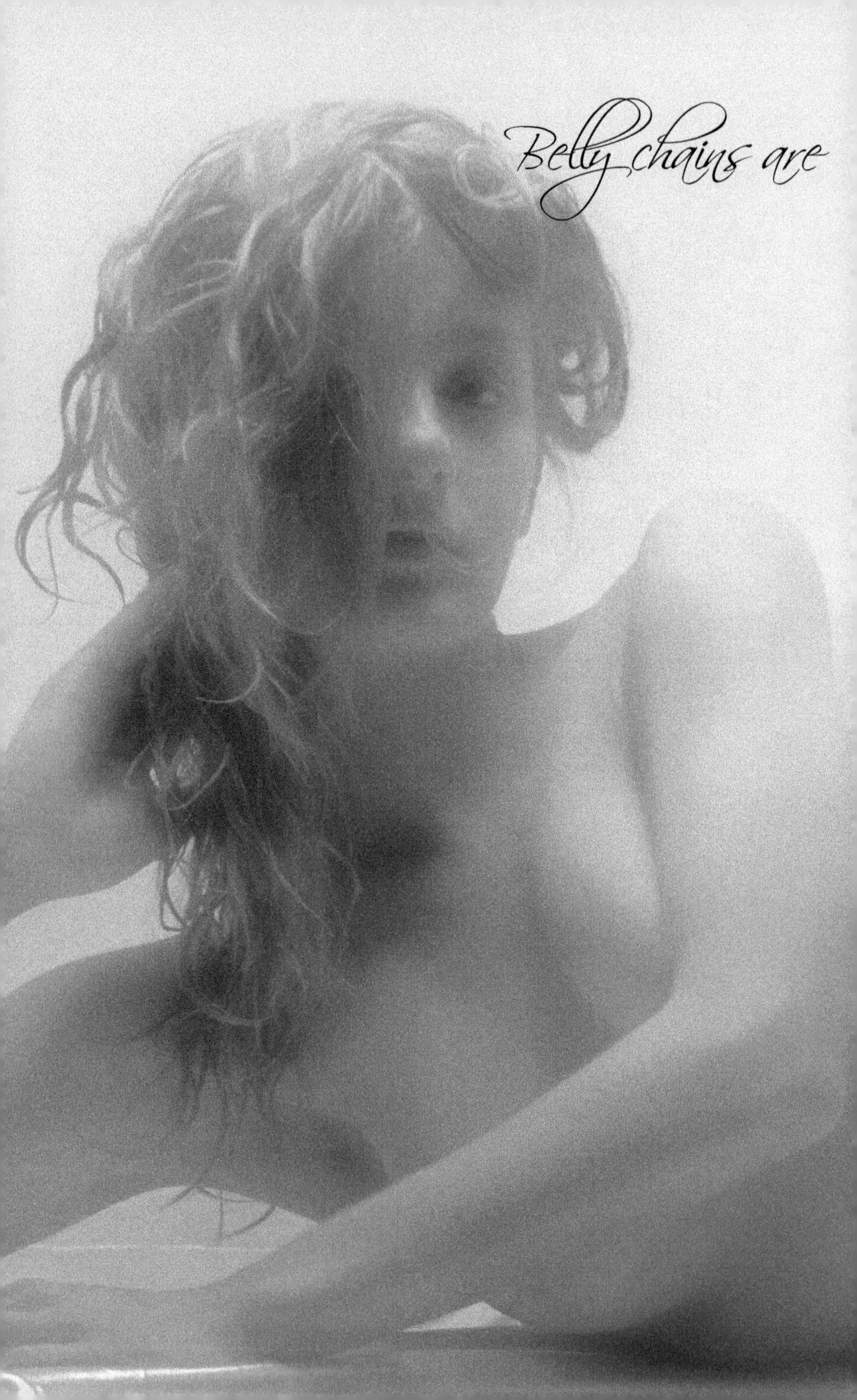

Belly chains are

the ultimate accessory.

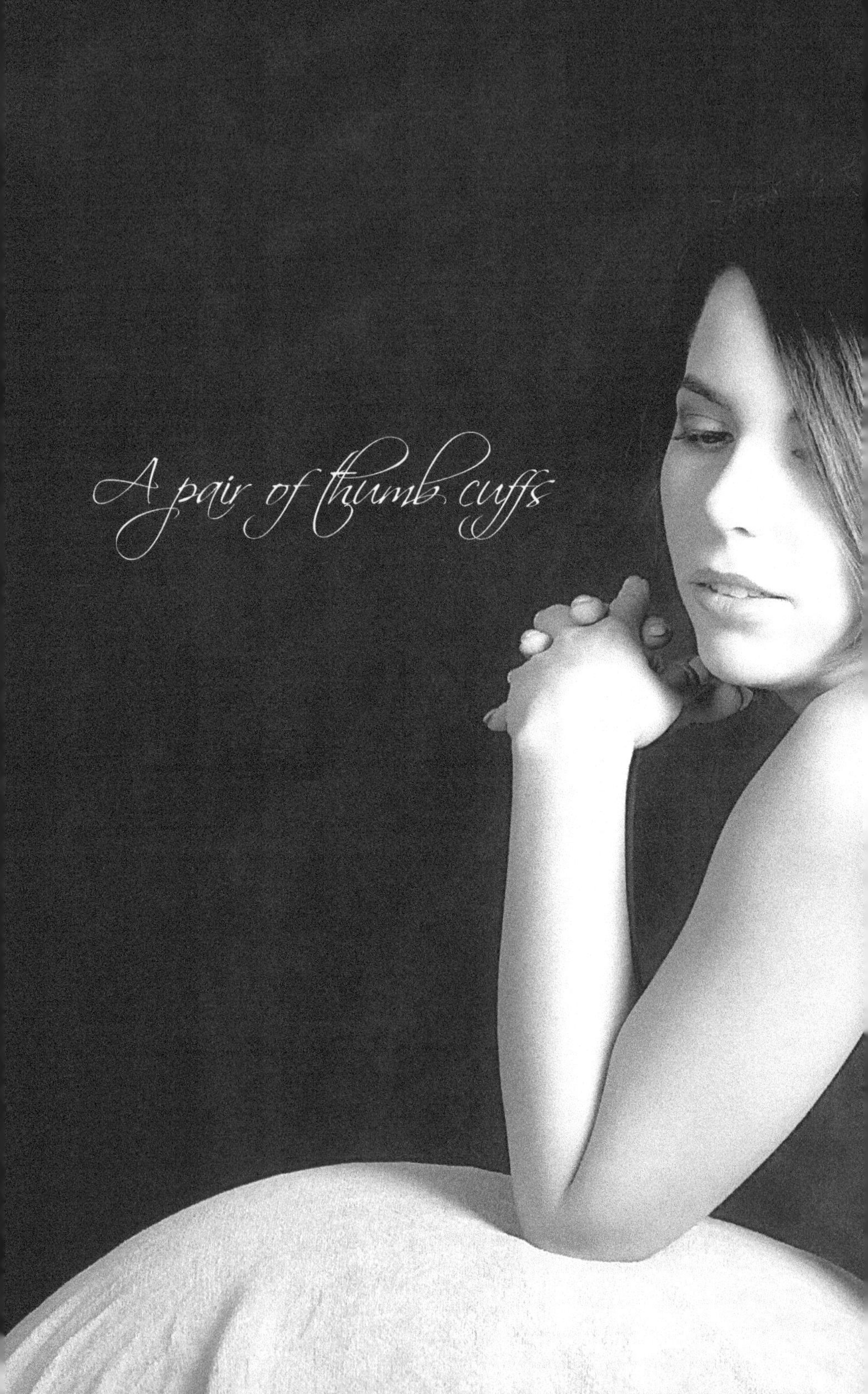
A pair of thumb cuffs

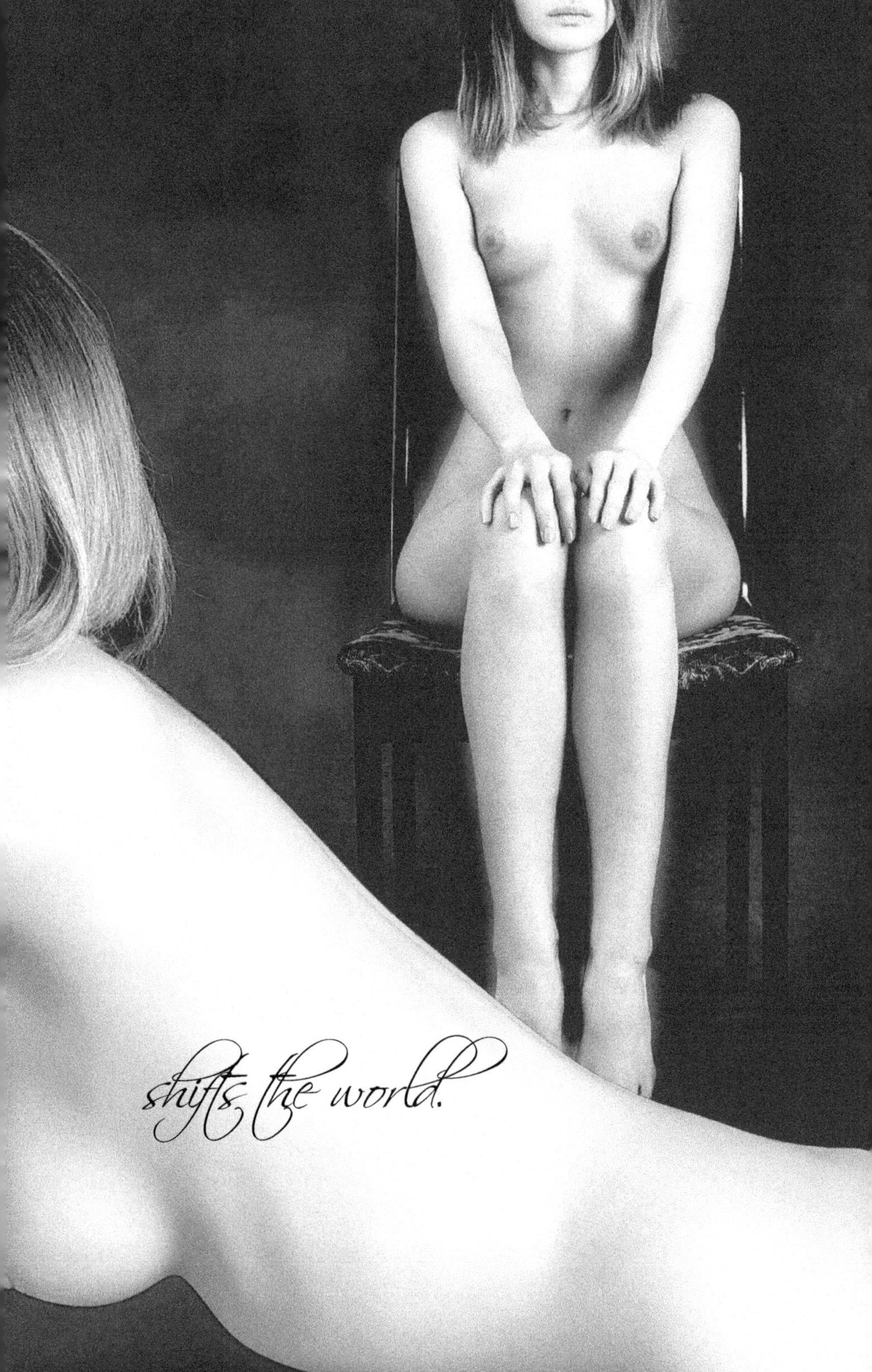
shifts the world.

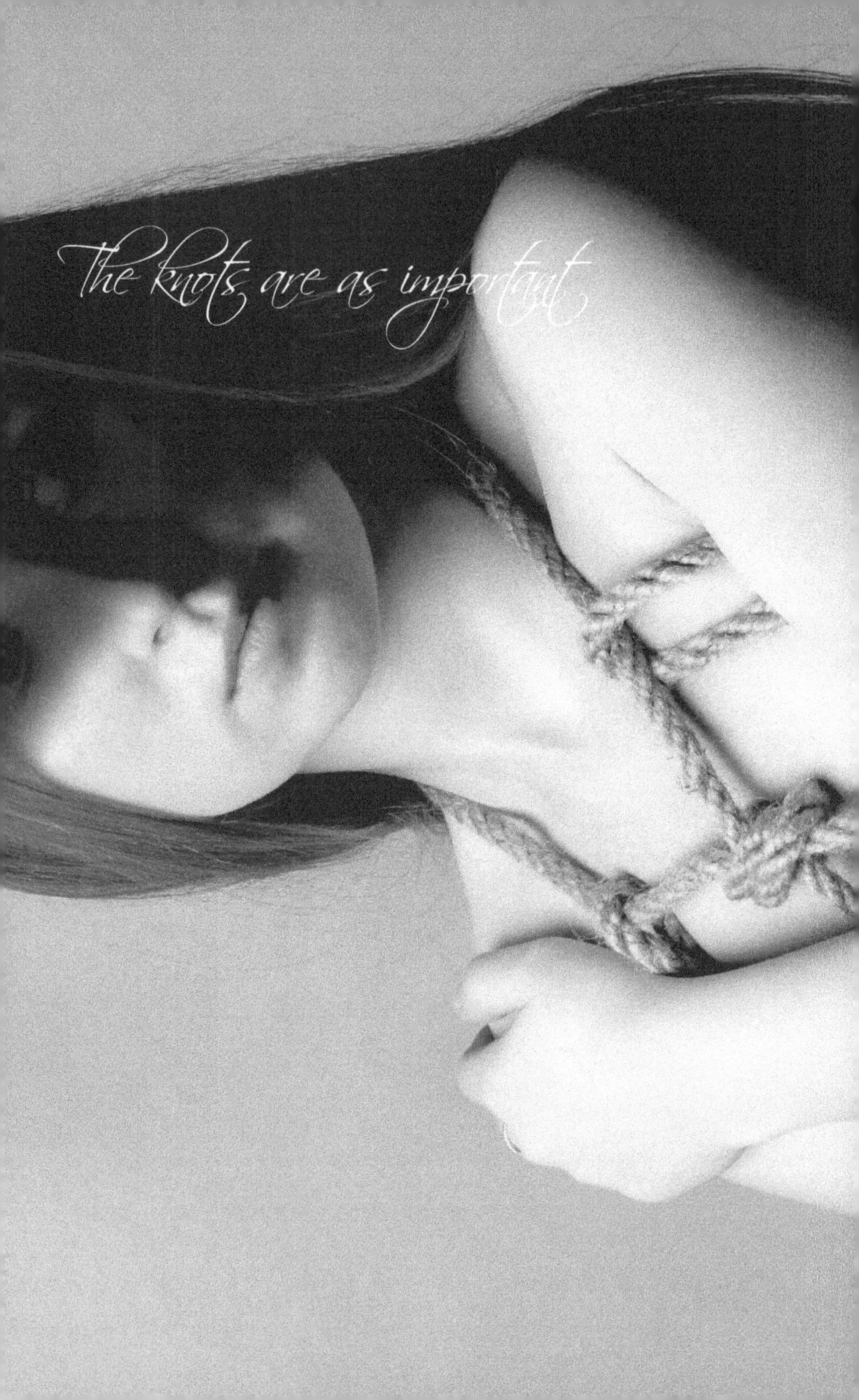

The knots are as important

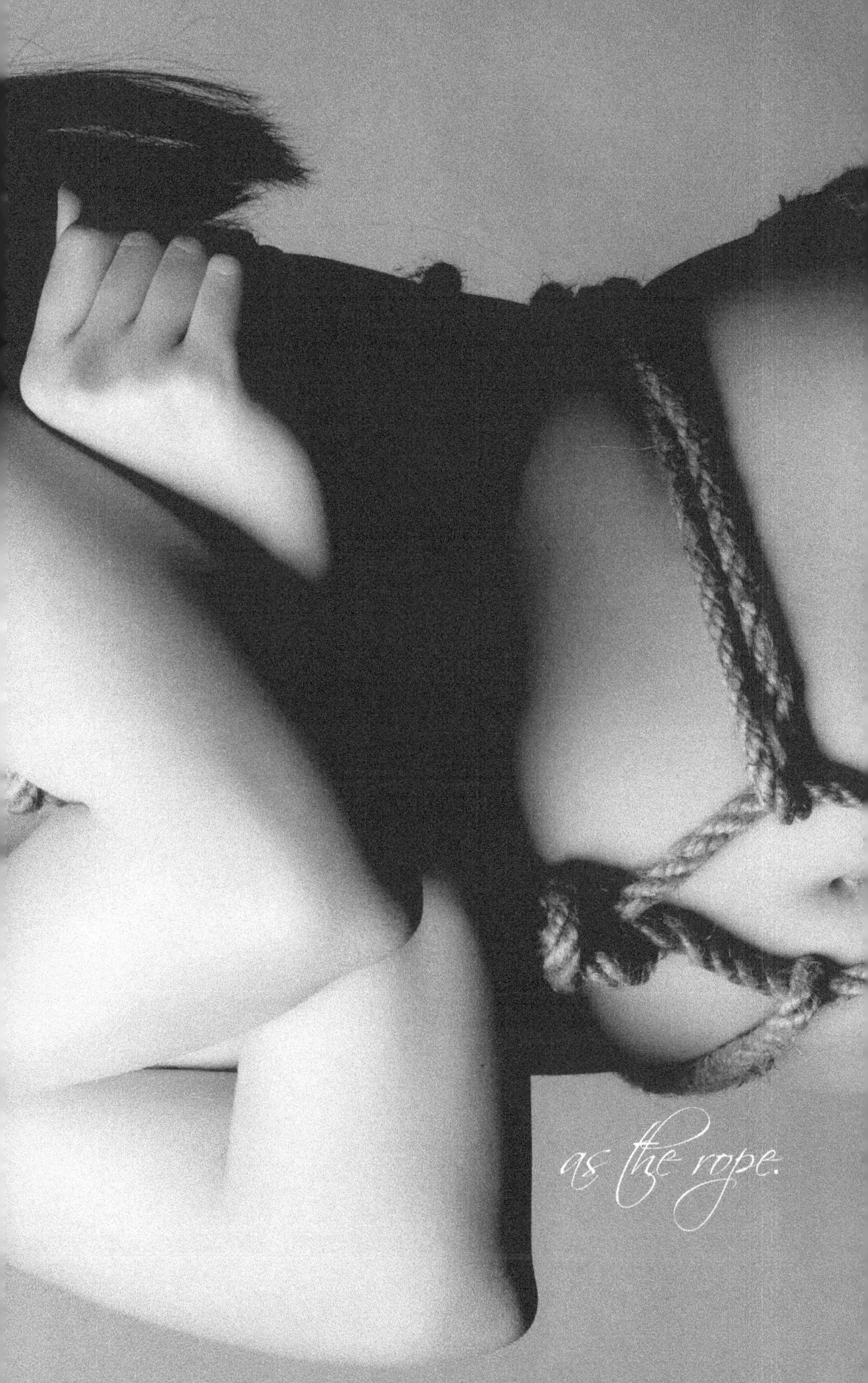
as the rope.

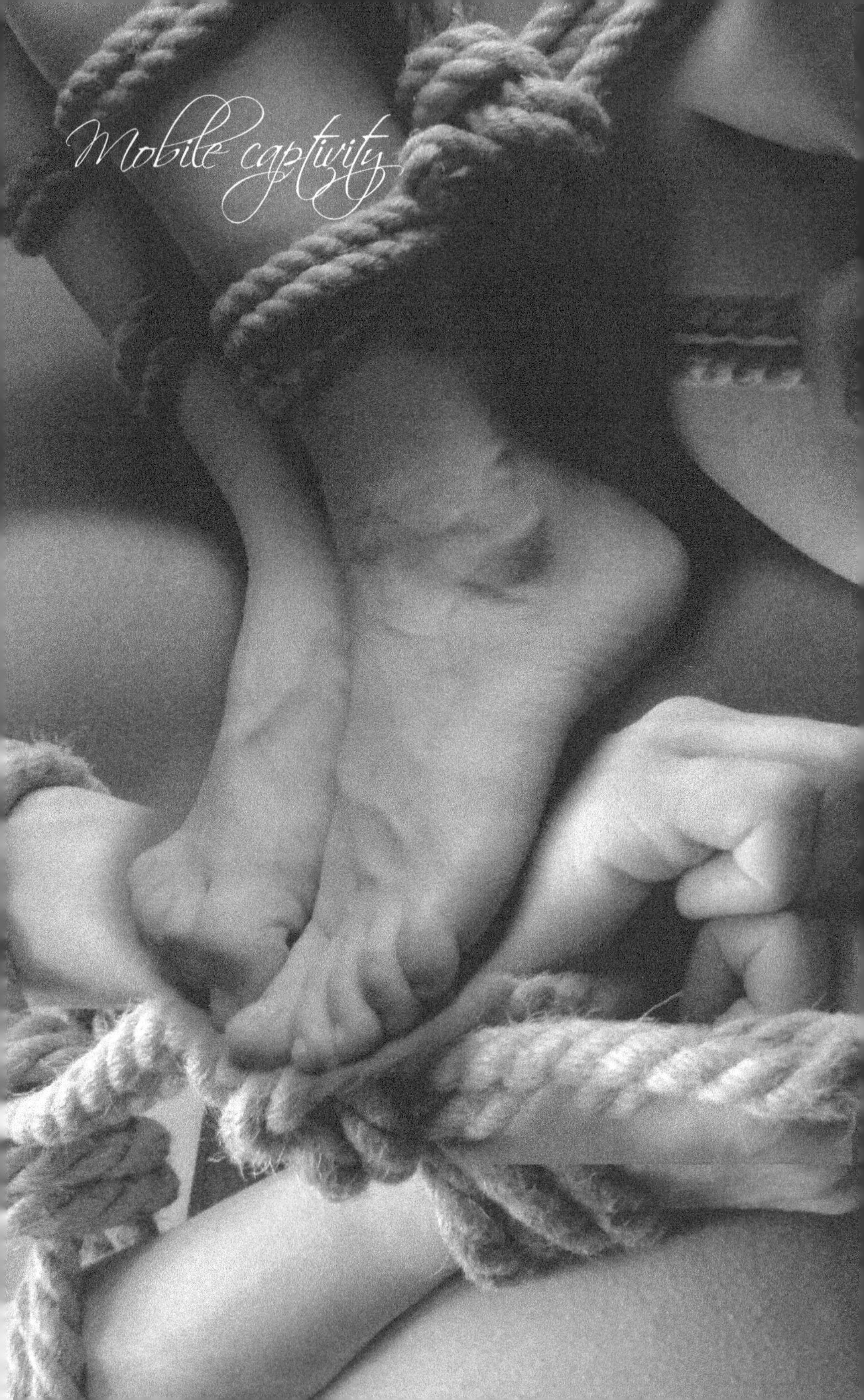
Mobile captivity

expands possibilities.

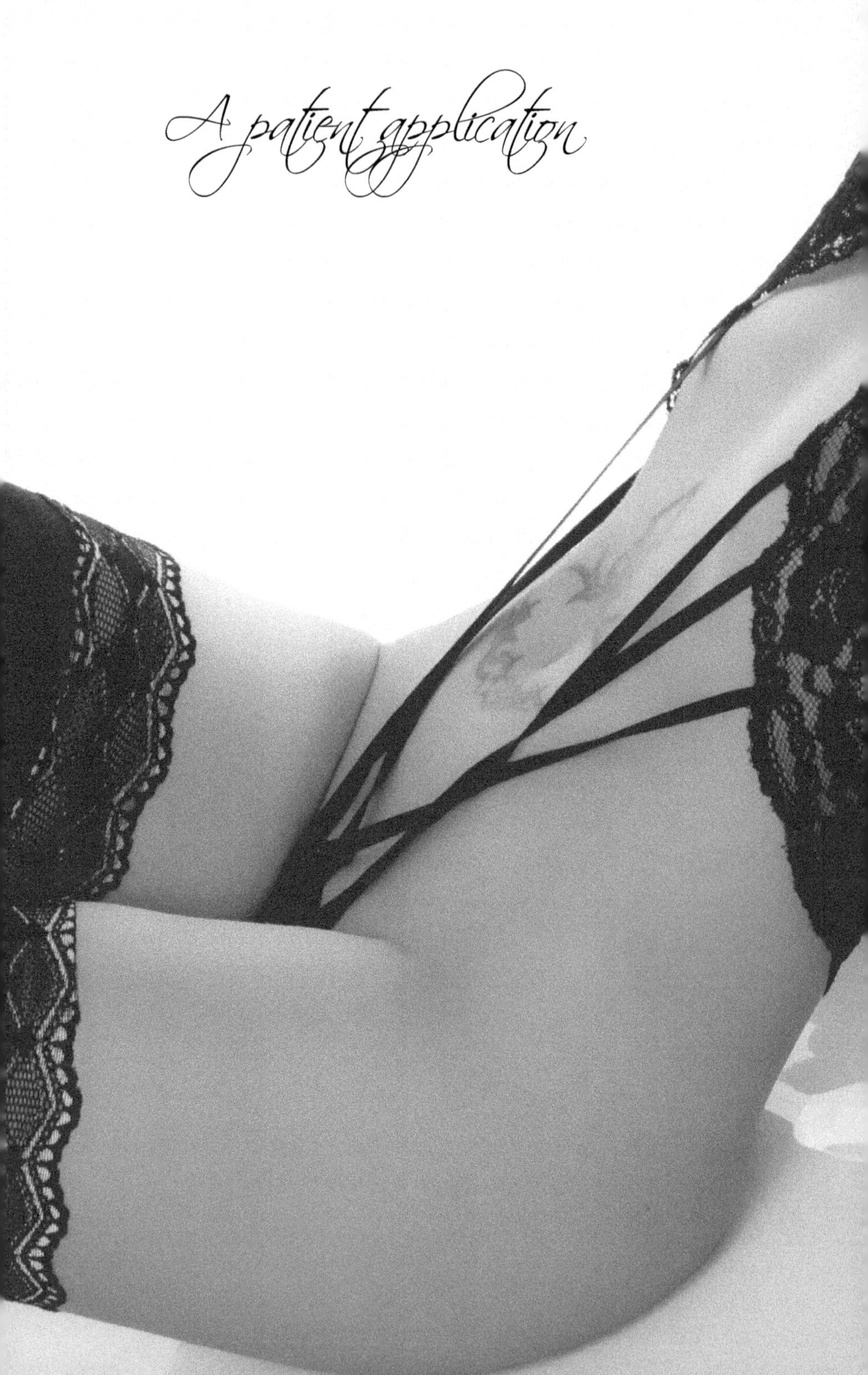
A patient application

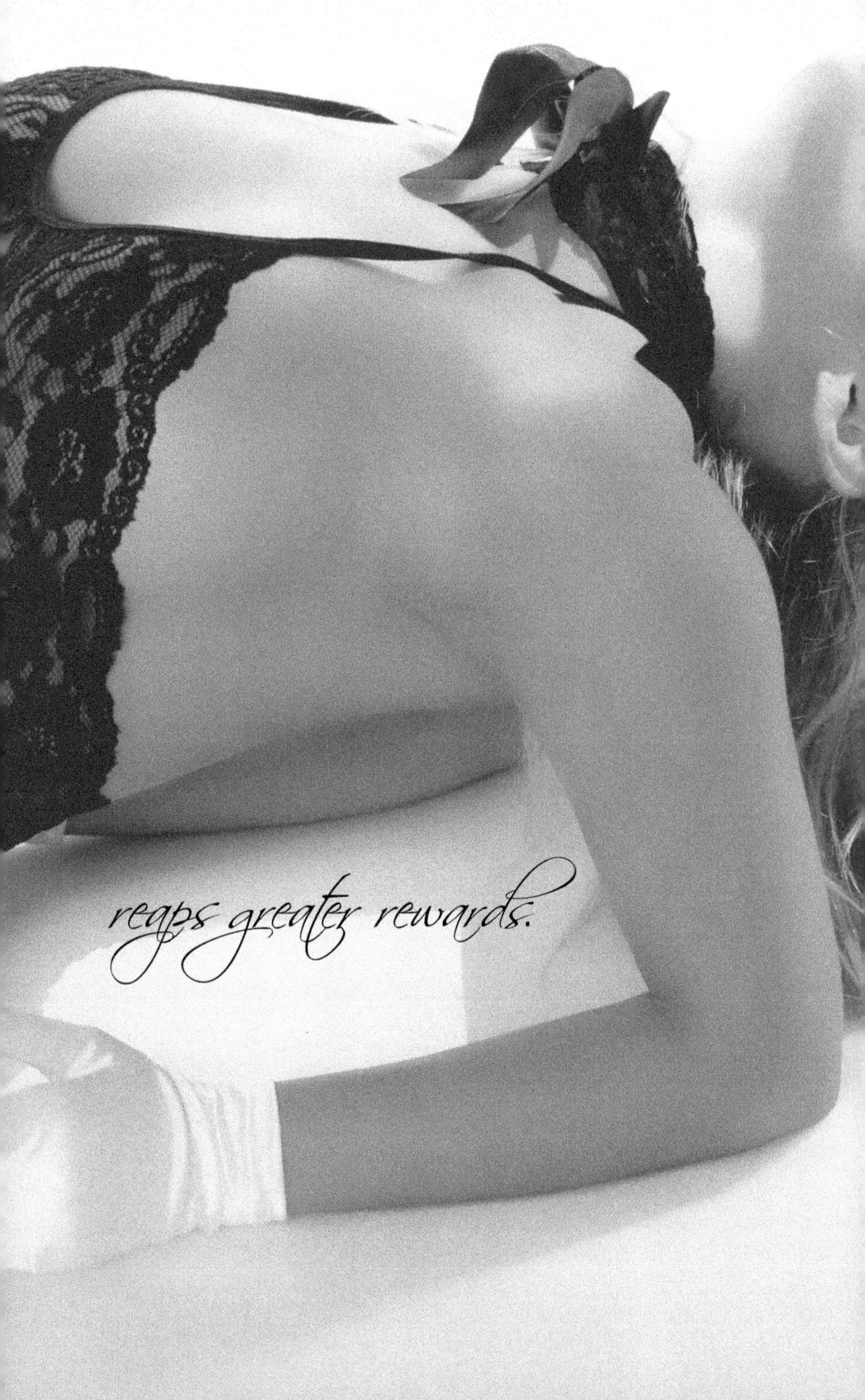
reaps greater rewards.

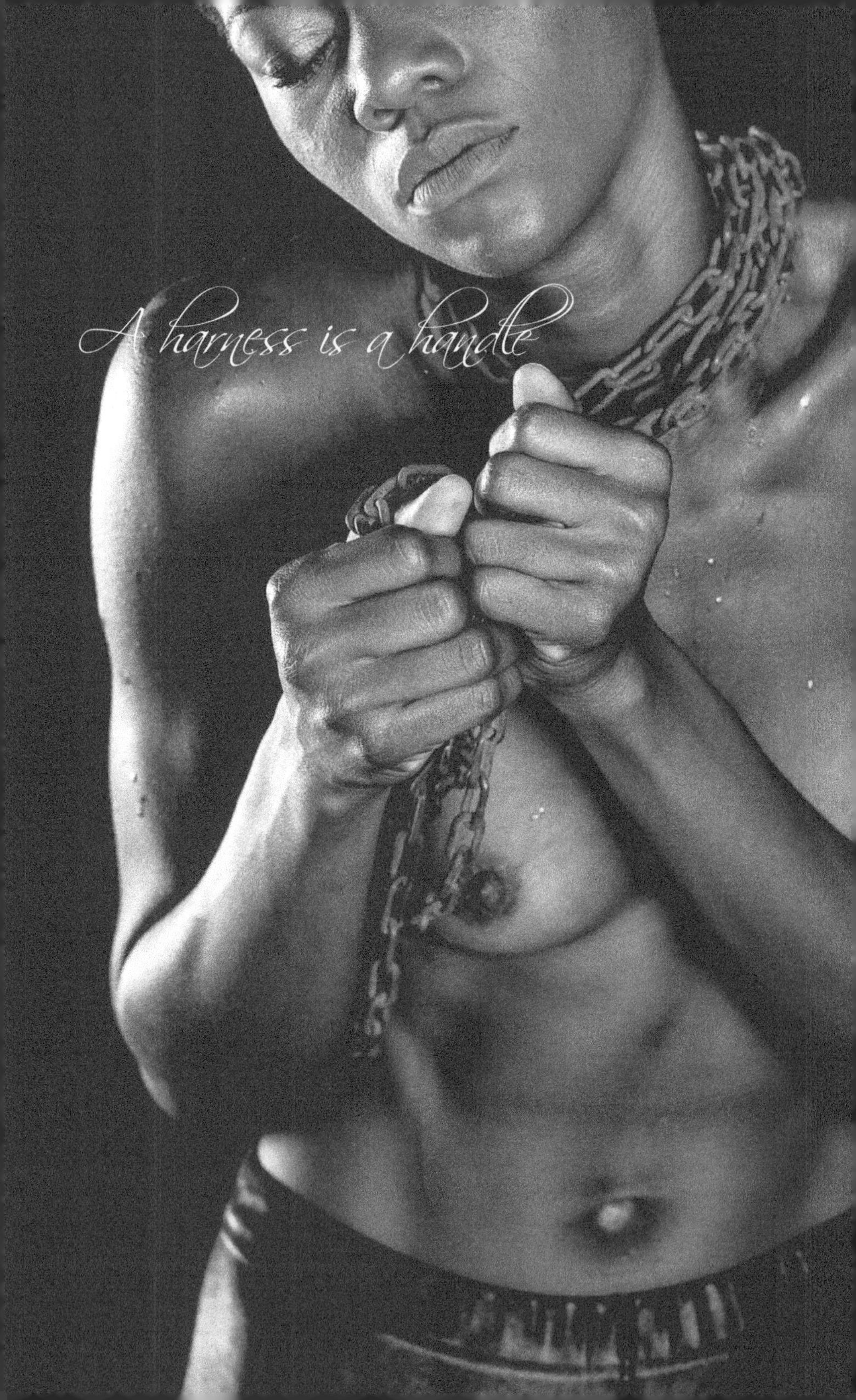

A harness is a handle

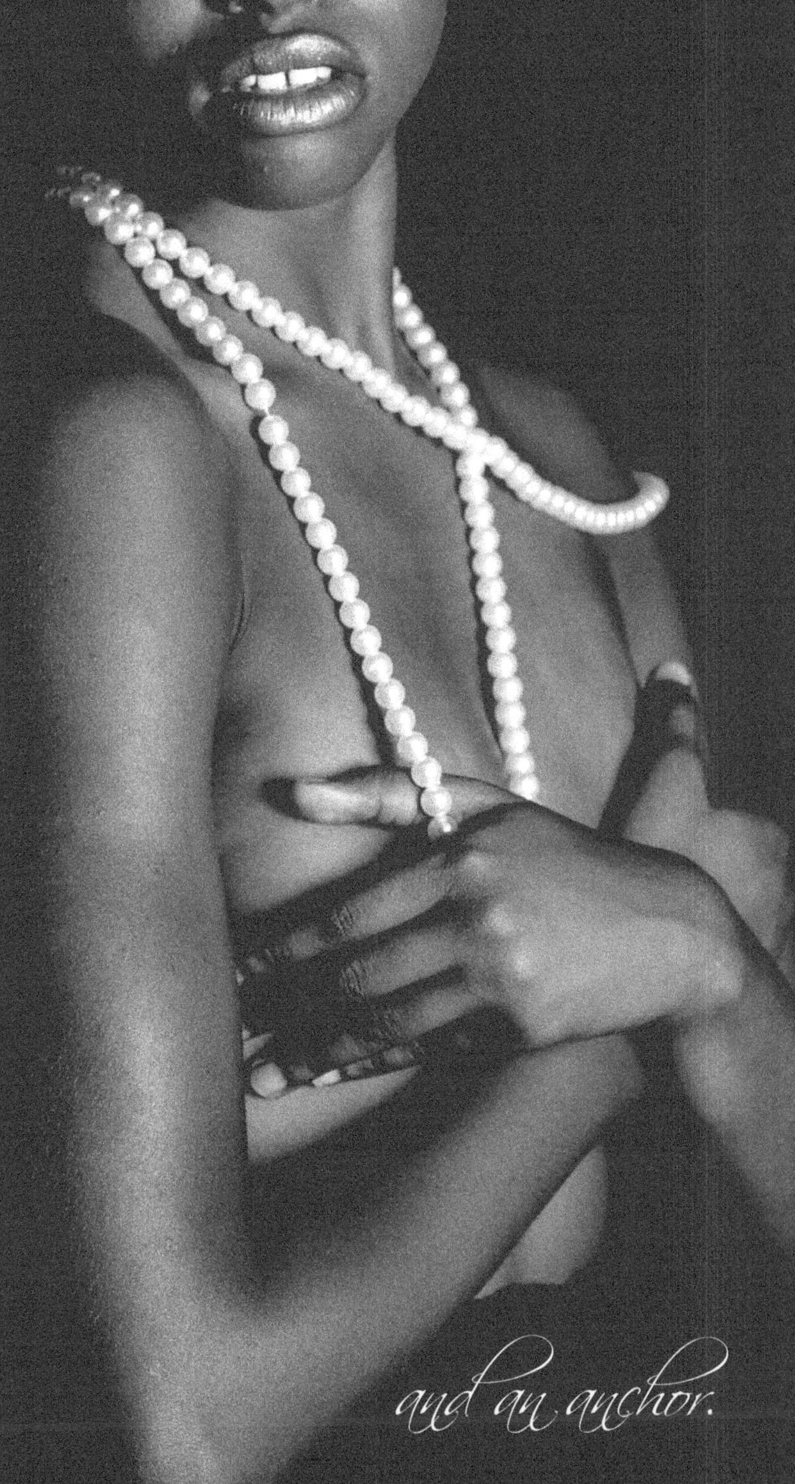
and an anchor.

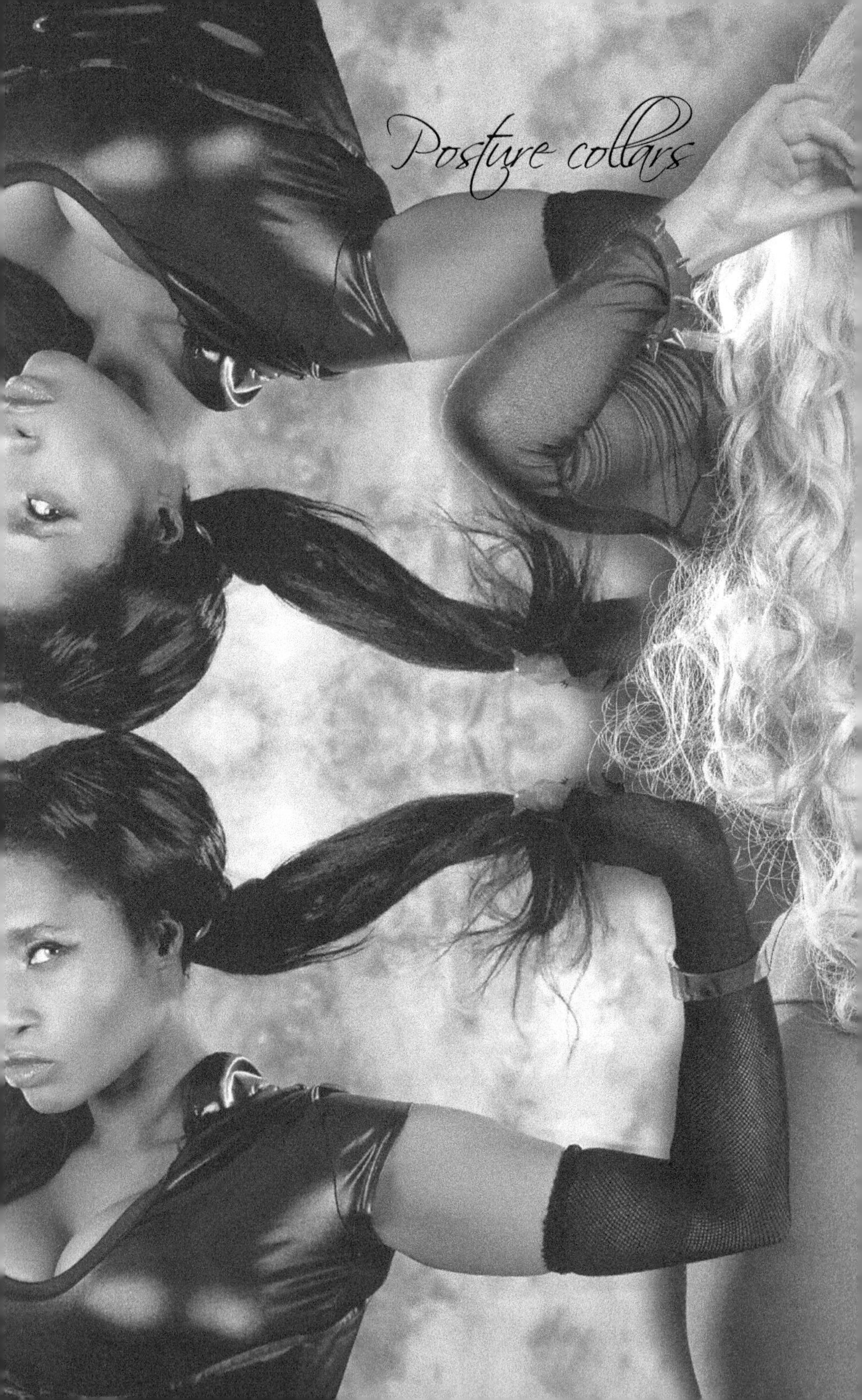
Posture collars

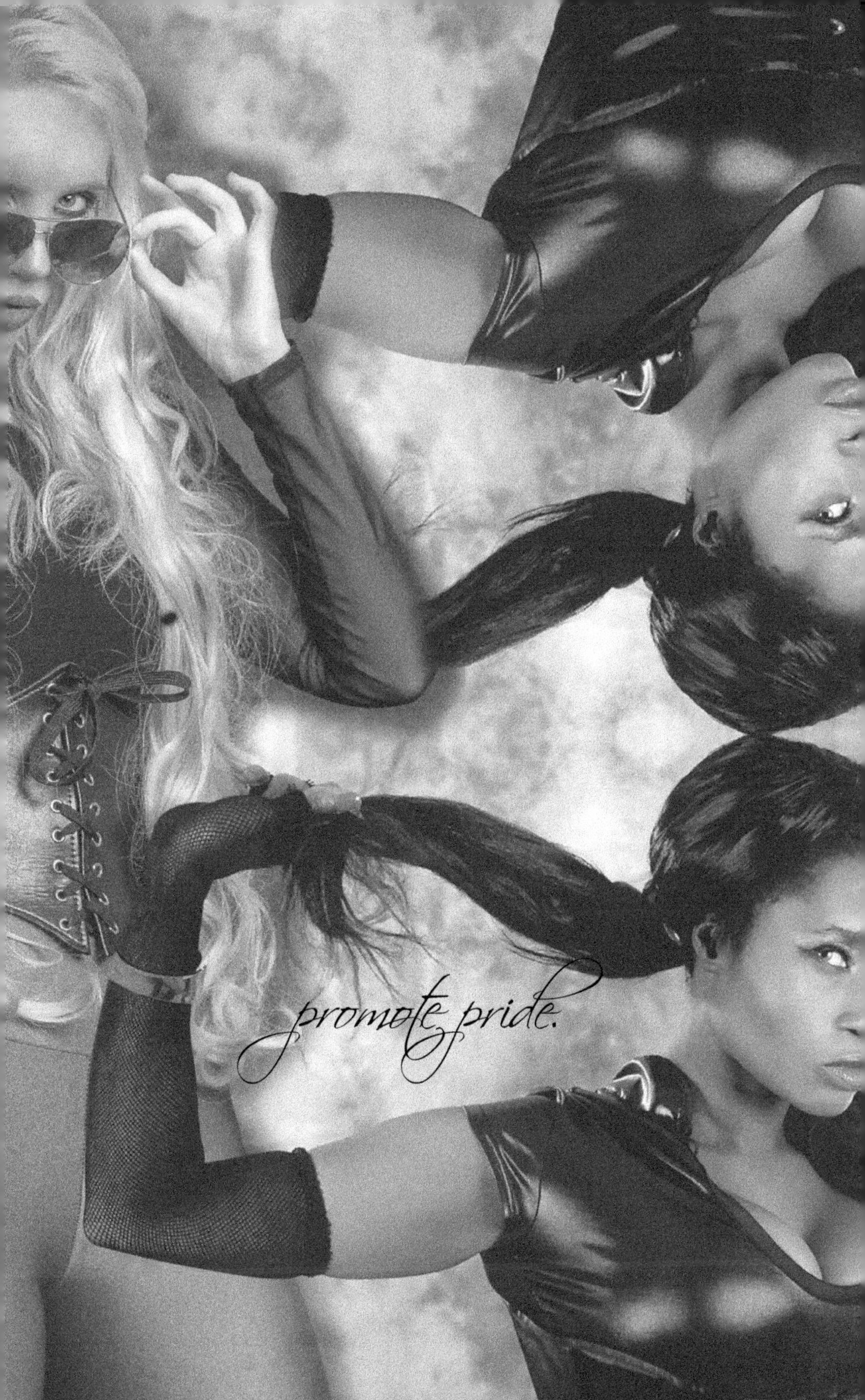
promote pride.

Being ensnared

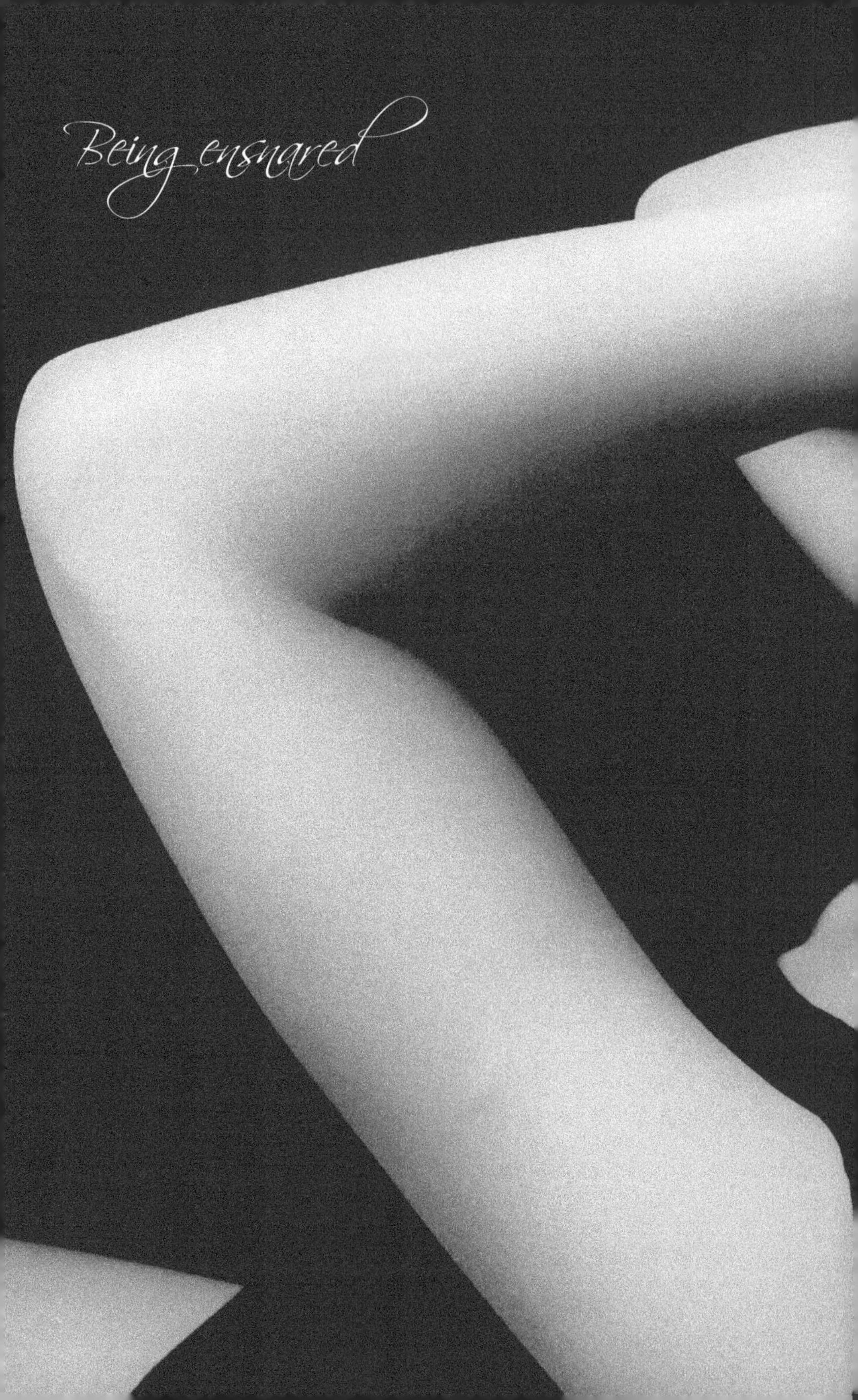

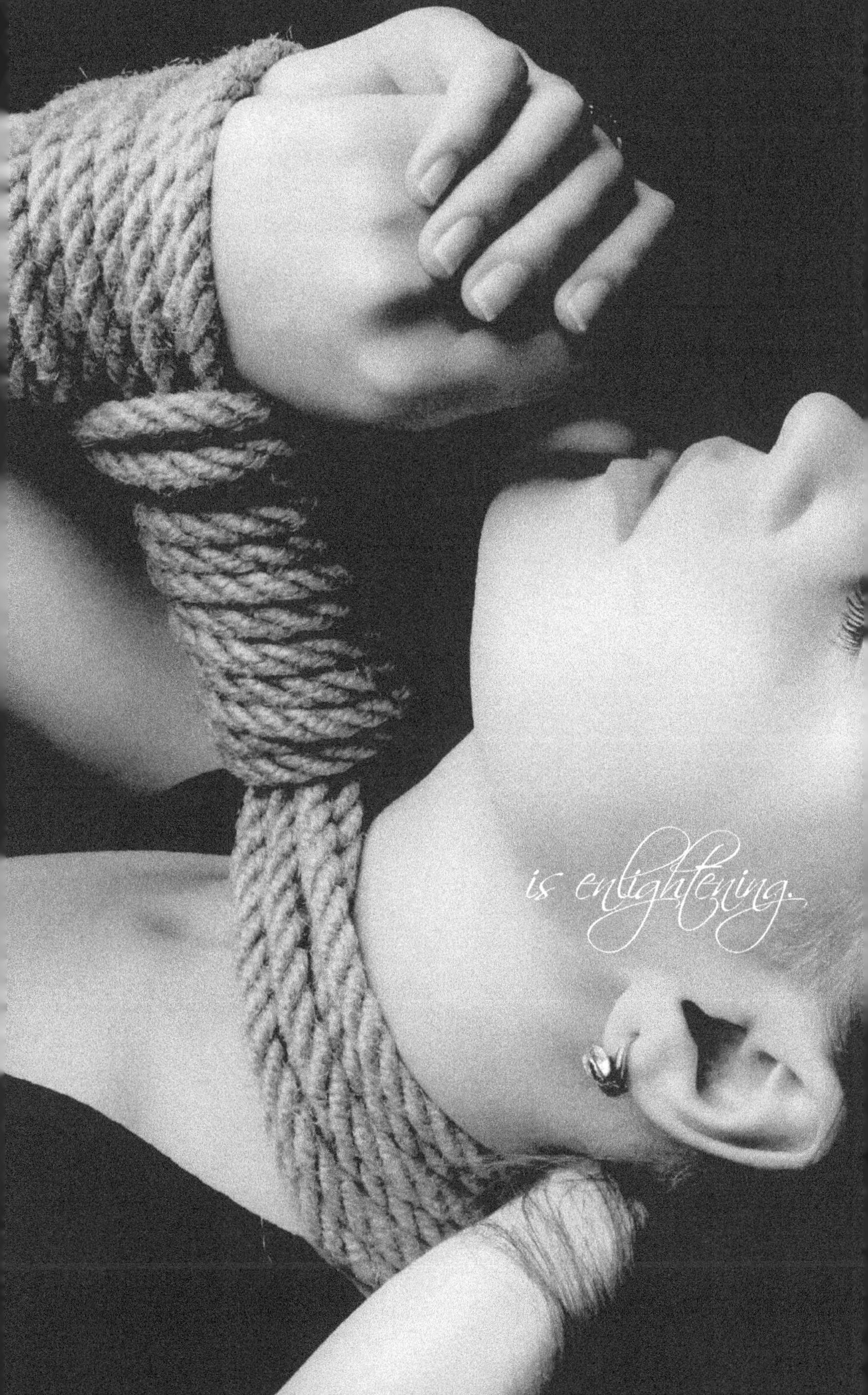
is enlightening.

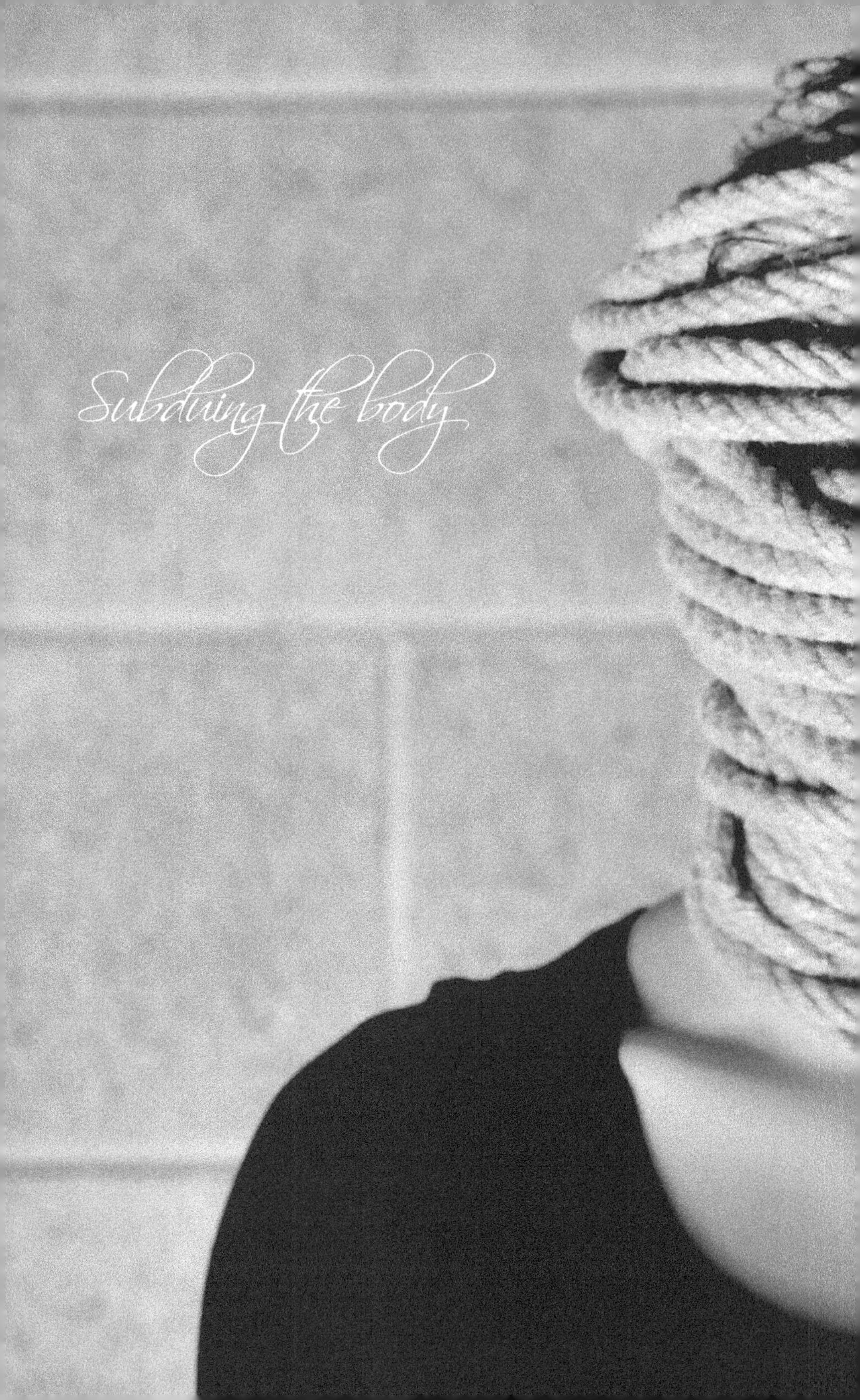

Subduing the body

subdues the mind.

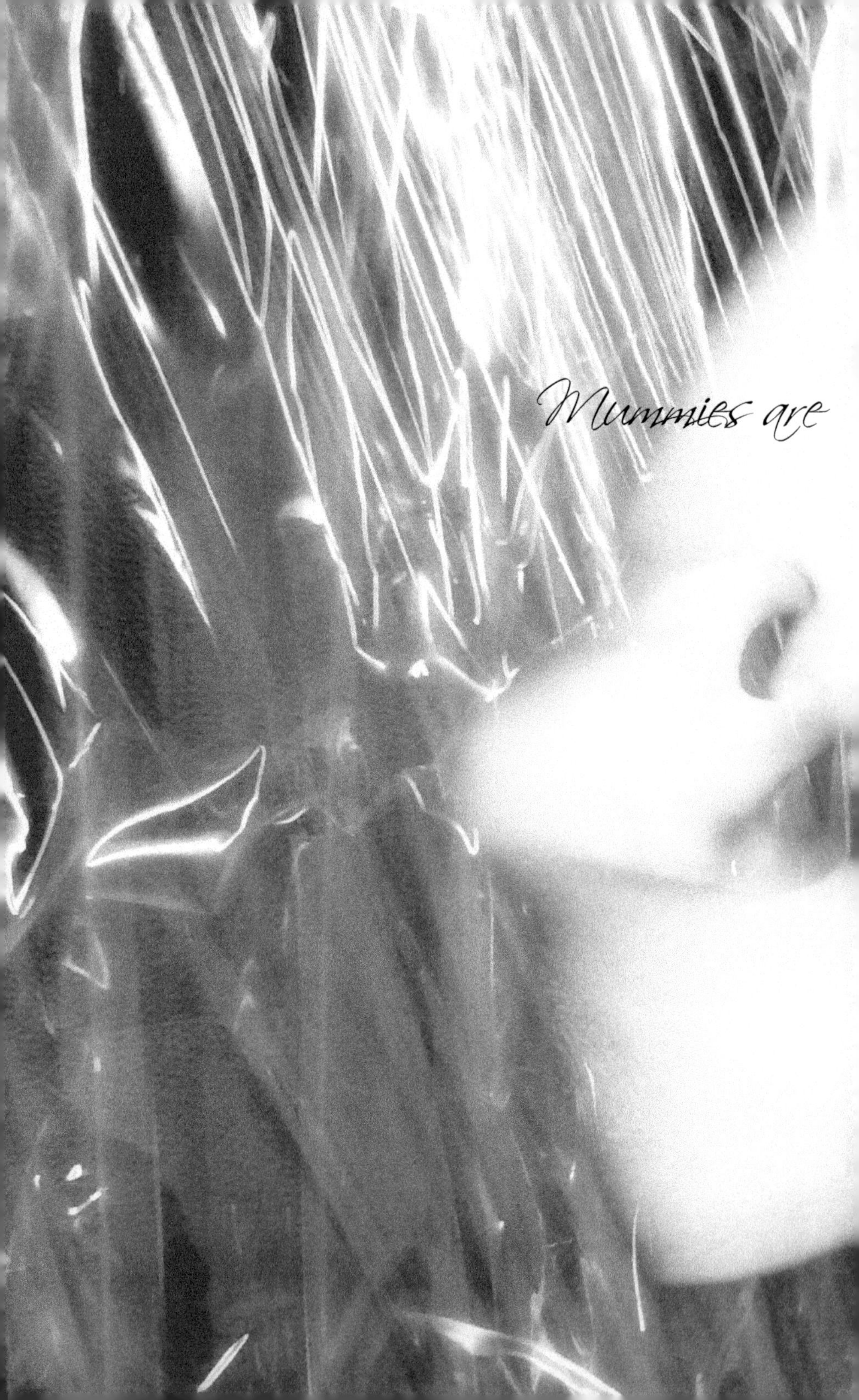
Mummies are

magnificent.

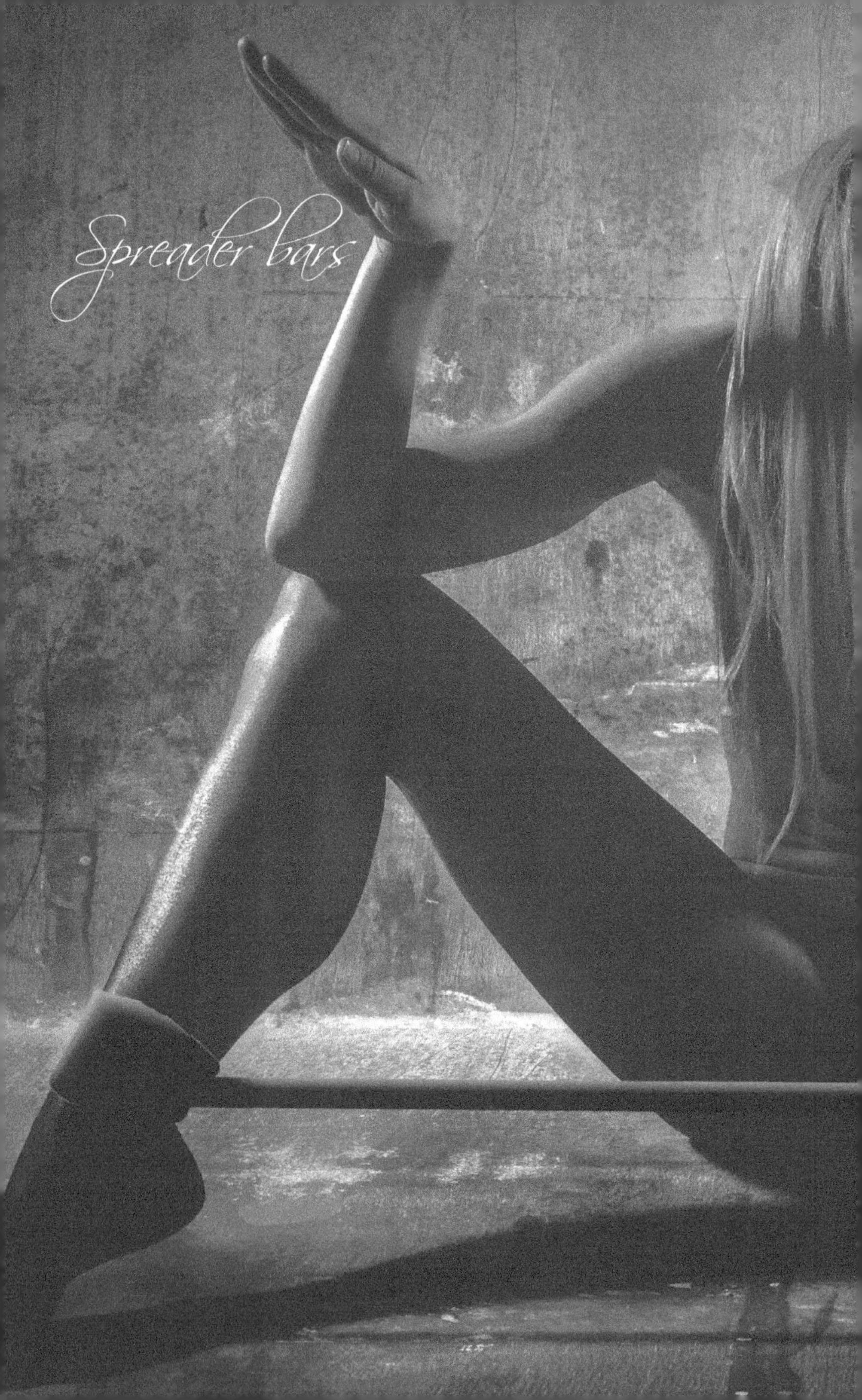

Spreader bars

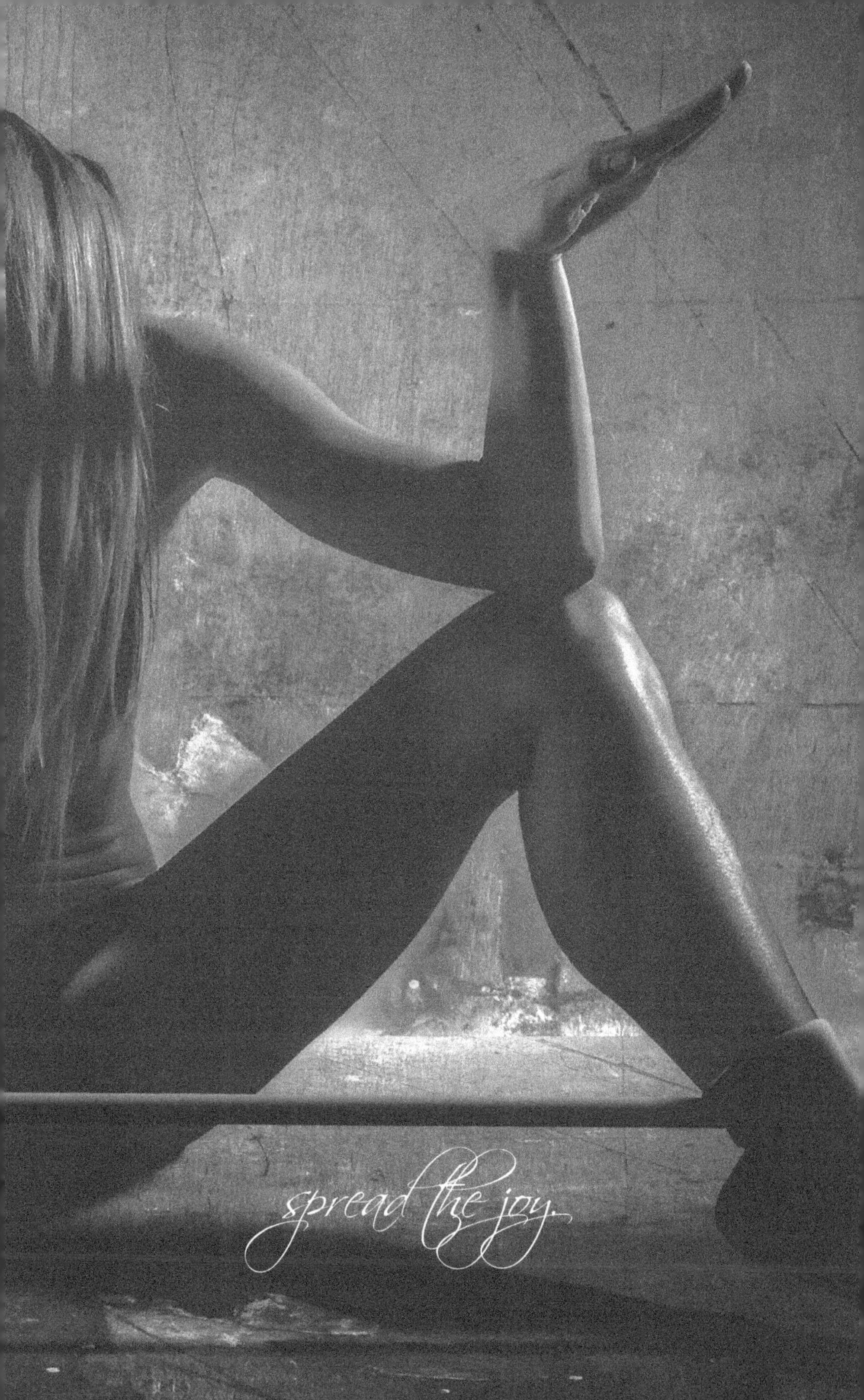
spread the joy.

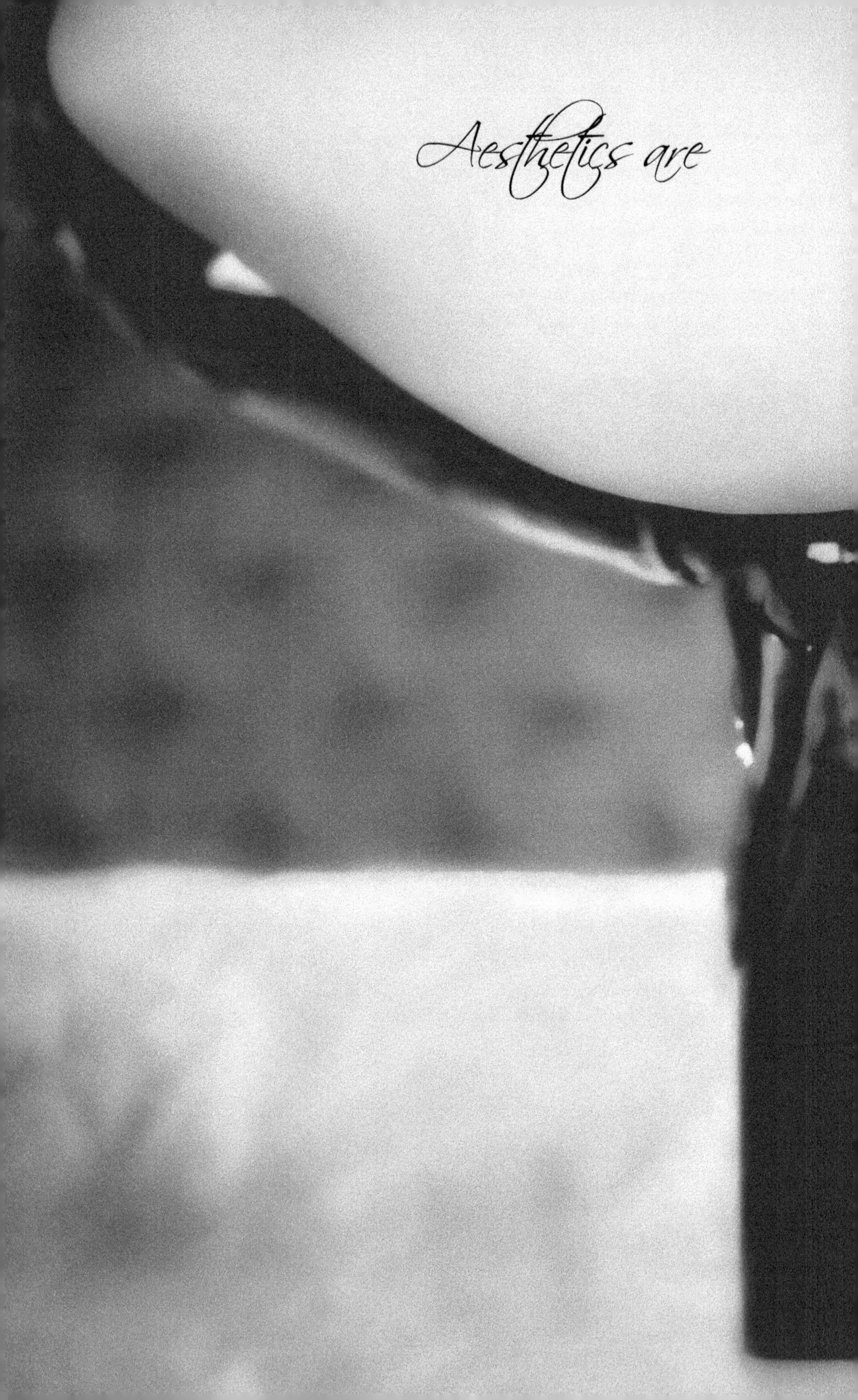

Aesthetics are

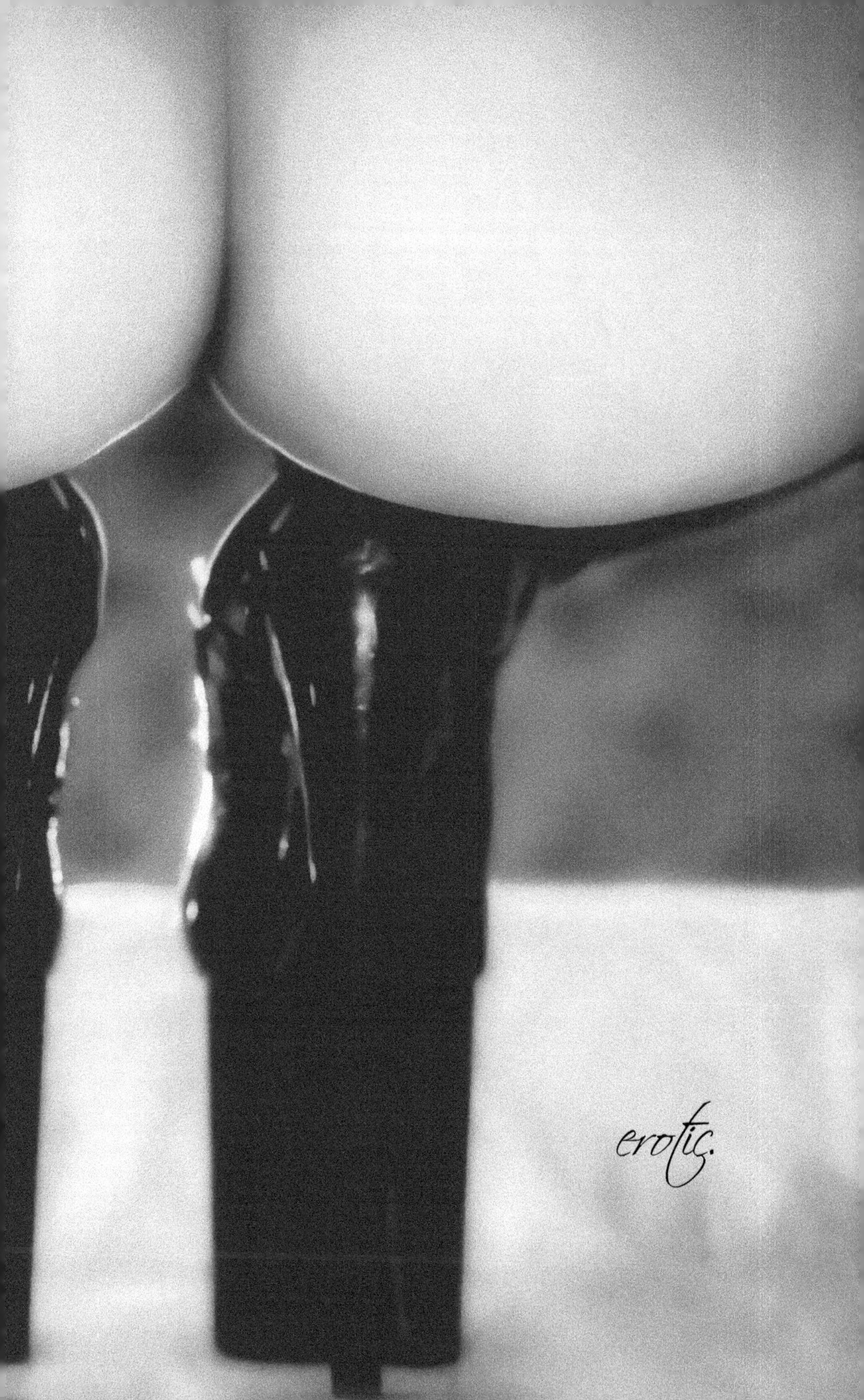
erotic.

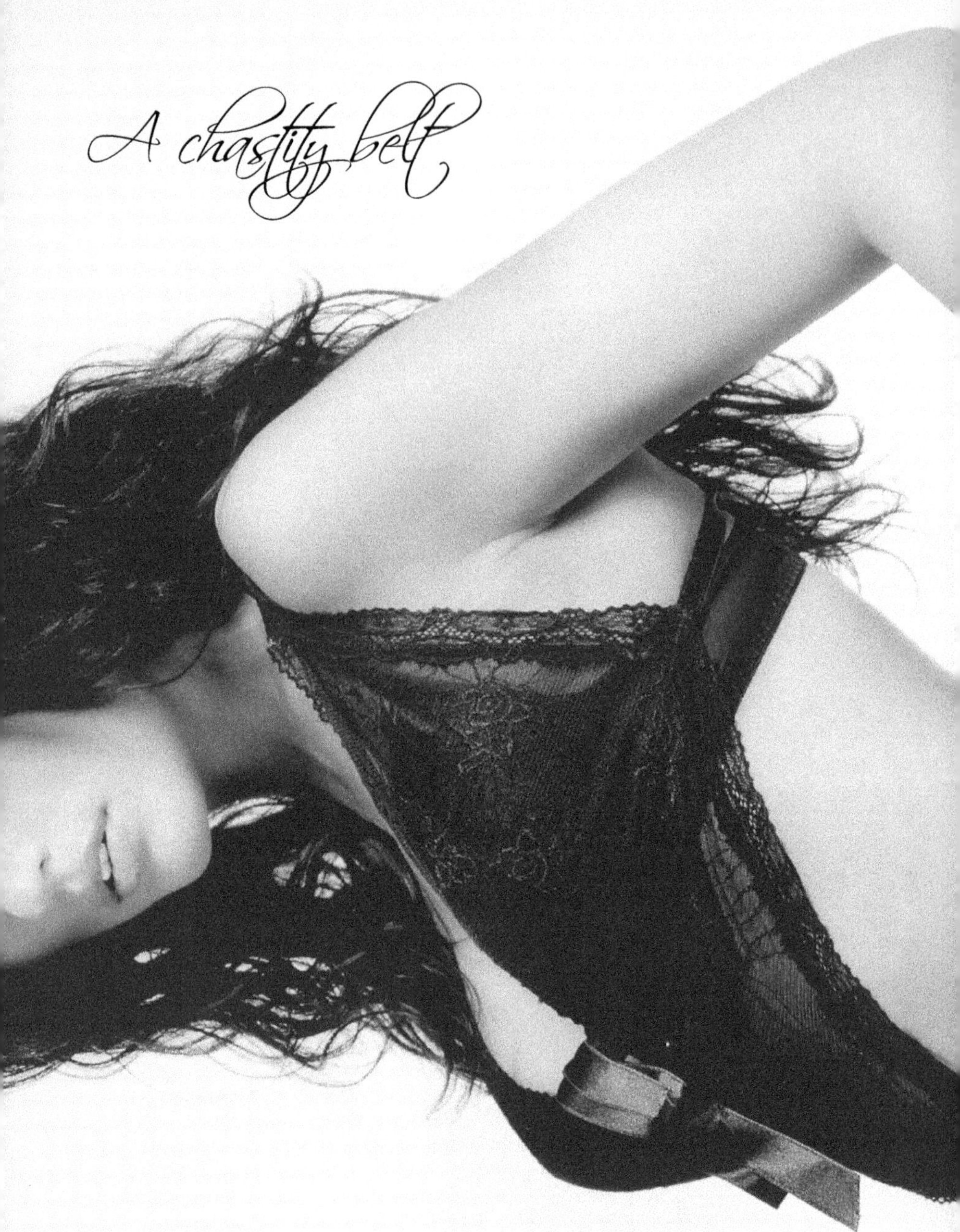
A chastity belt

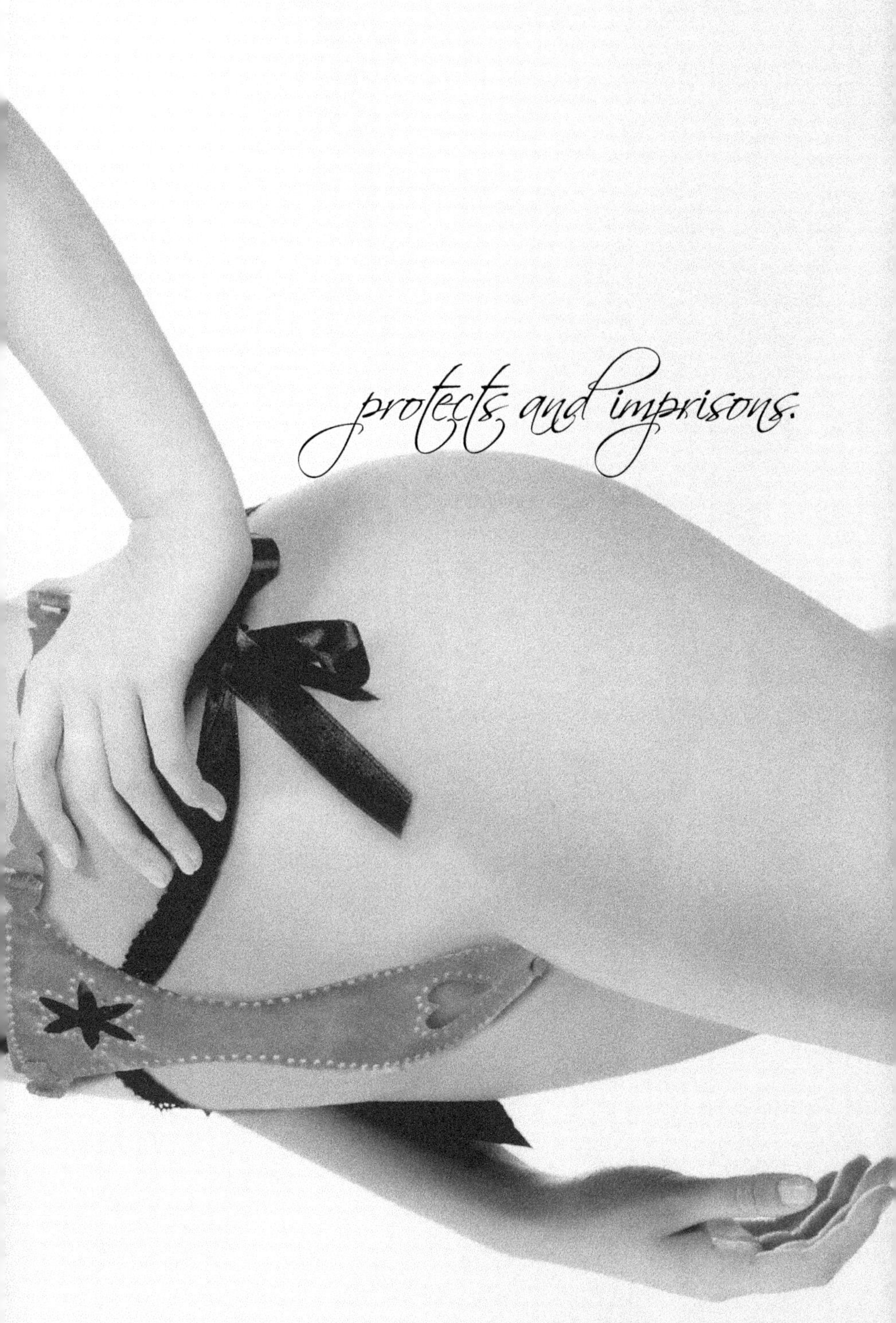
protects and imprisons.

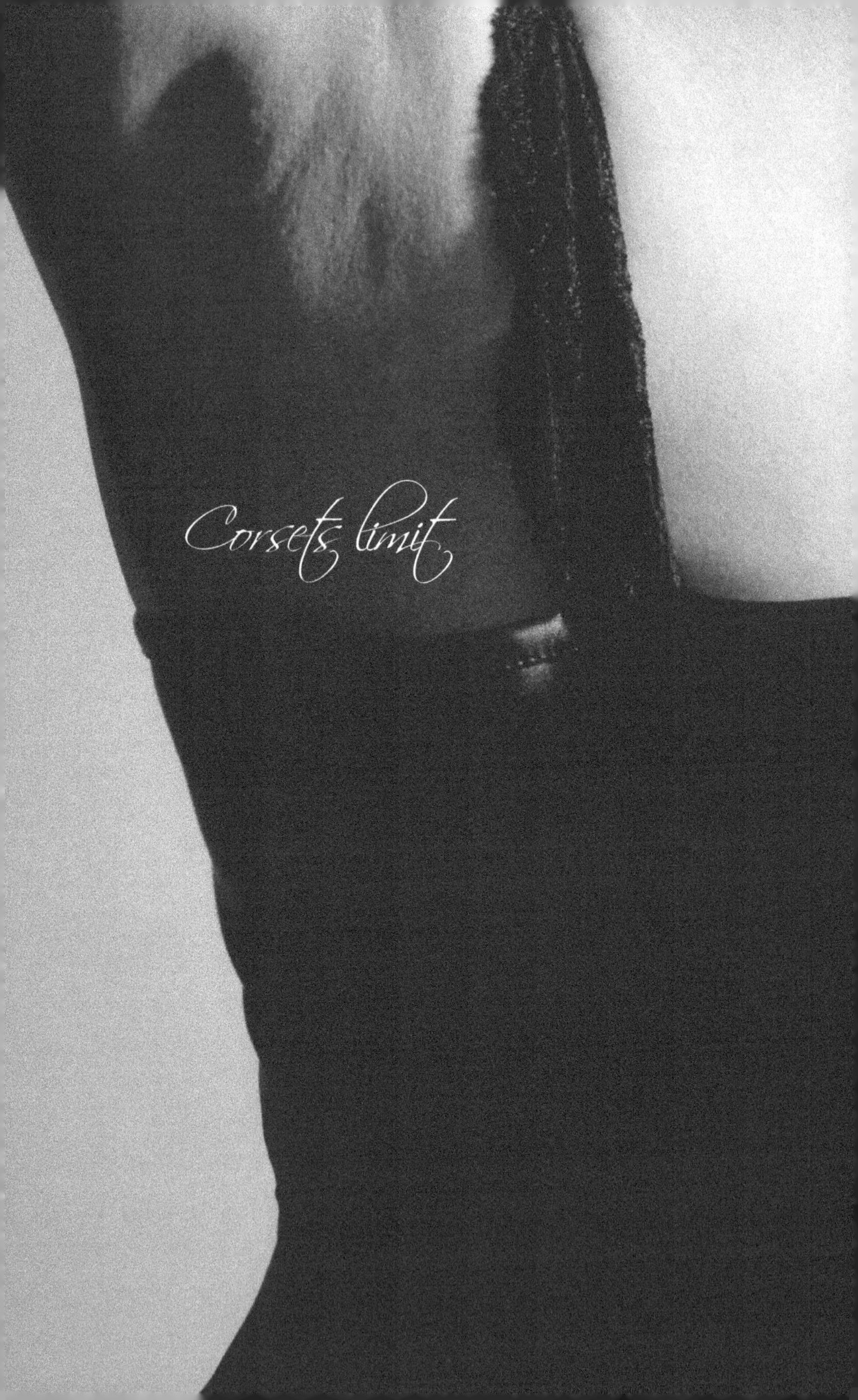

Corsets limit

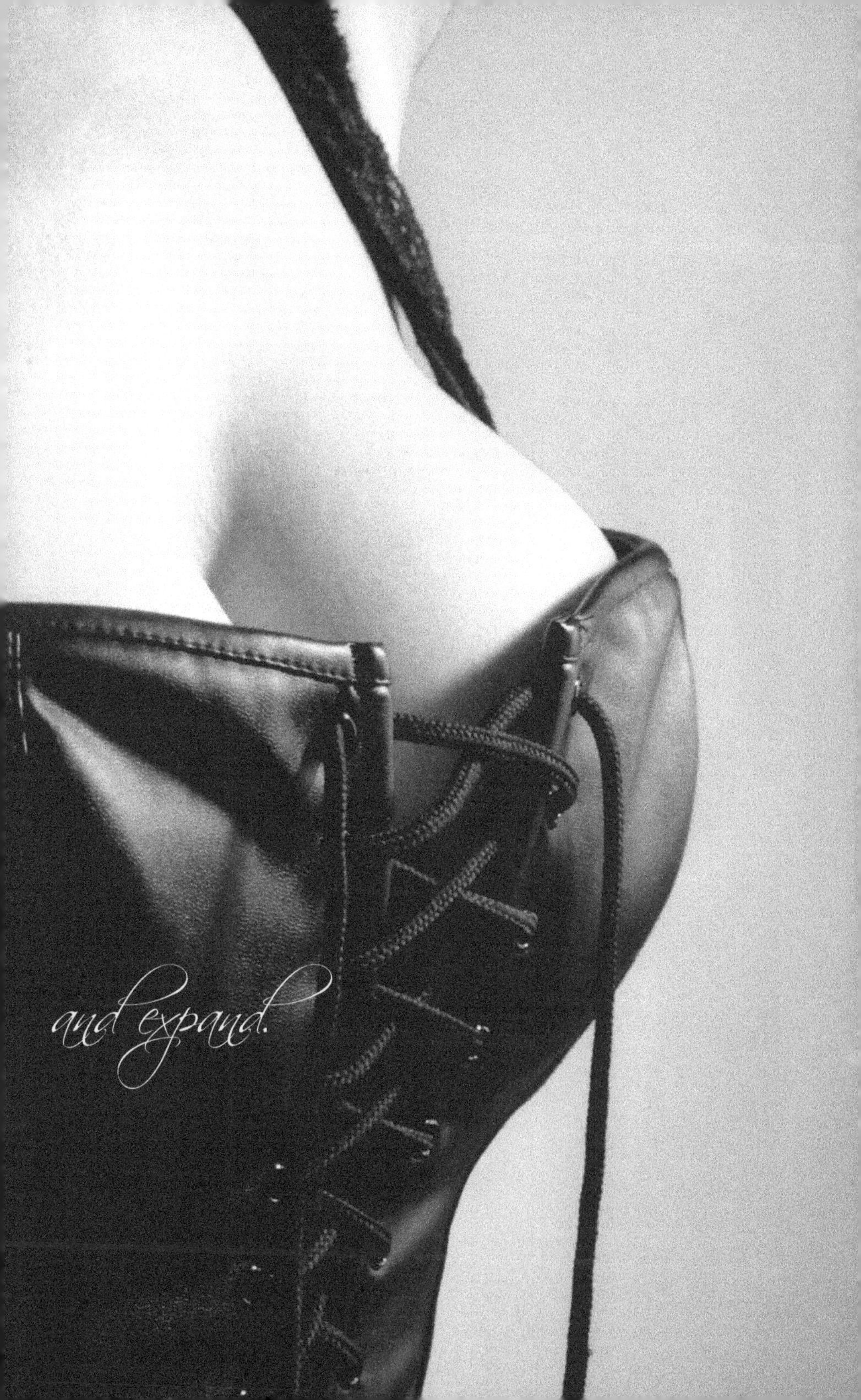
and expand.

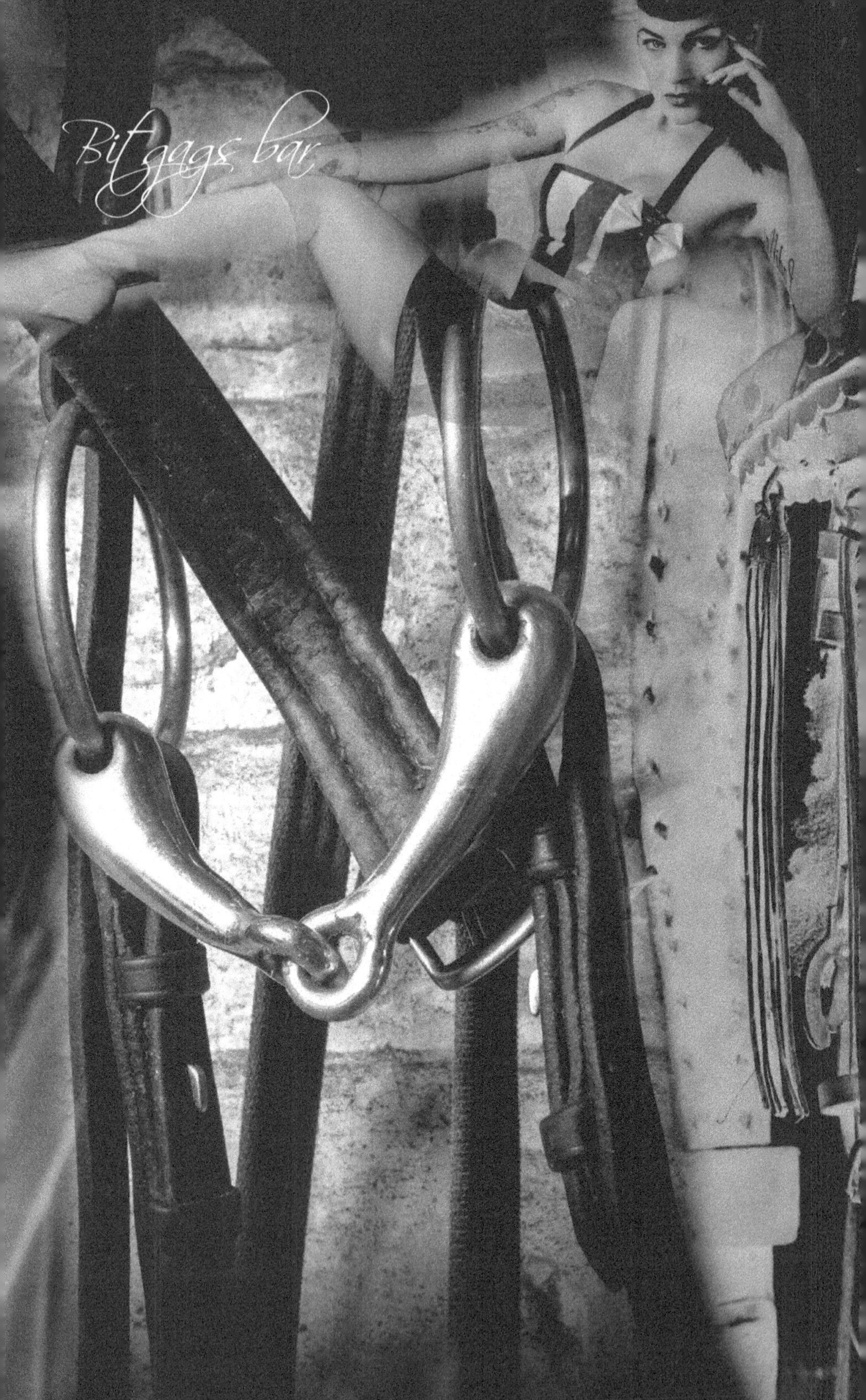
Bit gags bar

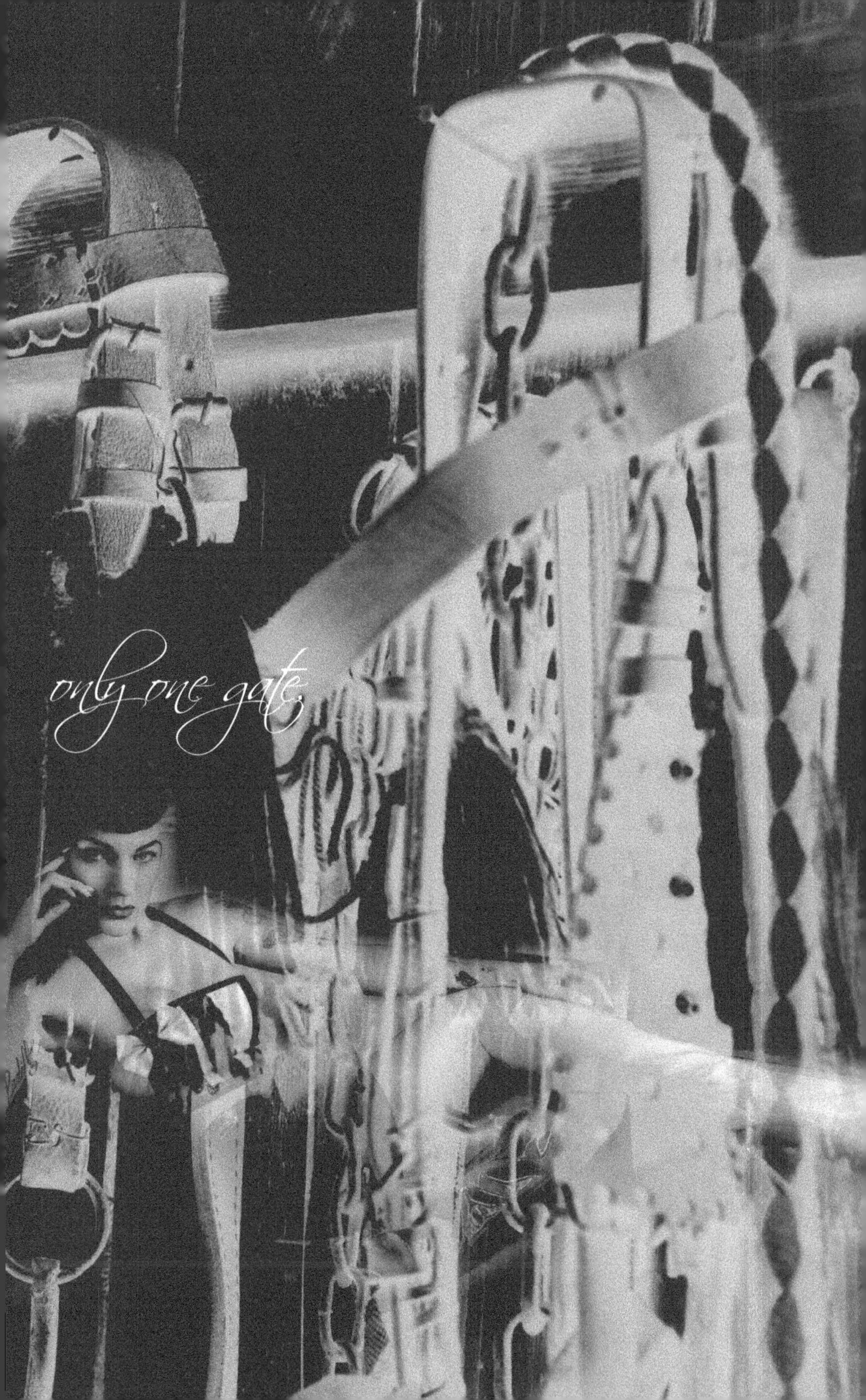
only one gate.

The Tao of Naughty Series

The Tao of Sex
An Erotic Bedside Companion

The Tao of BDSM
An Erotic Playtime Companion

The Tao of Bondage
An Erotic Binding Companion

www.ingramcontent.com/pod-product-compliance
Ingram Content Group UK Ltd.
Pitfield, Milton Keynes, MK11 3LW, UK
UKHW021528300726
14060UKWH00011B/19